Wounded Deer Leaps Highest

Vima Dasan, S.J.

To
Mr. Chukles

Fr. Dasan sj

DEDICATION
to the Blessed Virgin Mary,
Our Lady of Walsingham

Decani Books

Wounded Deer Leaps Highest first published in 1996 by Decani Books, 30 North Terrace, Mildenhall, Suffolk IP28 7AB

© 1996 Vima Dasan, S.J.

Cover Design © Roy Cleaver

Cum permissu superiorum

ISBN 1 900 31402 9

ACKNOWLEDGMENTS

Extracts from the Book of Common Prayer, the rights of which are vested in the Crown, are reproduced by permission of the Crown's Patentee, Cambridge University Press.

Prayer by Donald Hilton by permission of McCrimmon Publishing Co Lrd.

Extracts from the *The Roman Missal* © 1973 International Committee on English in the Liturgy, Inc. (I.C.E.L.); from the *Rite of Christian Initiation of Adults* © 1985 I.C.E.L.; and *Our Father, we have wandered* from the *Resource Collection of Hymns and Service Music for the Liturgy* © 1981, I.C.E.L.

Lord Graciously Hear Us © Anne Conway.

Printed and bound by RPM Reprographics, 2-3 Spur Road, Quarry Lane, Chichester, West Sussex, PO19 2PR

Contents

Foreword

Wounded Deer Leaps Highest is a series of reflection on the liturgy of the Word of God proclaimed on the Sundays of Advent and Lent in the three-year cycle. Pastors are called to break the Word of God as they do with the Bread of Life. There is a need to overcome the gap of centuries and geography and cultural chasms to understand God's Word today and to be nourished spiritually.

Fr Vima Dasan, an Indian Jesuit, has effectively used these reflections week after week to bring meaning, wisdom and inspiration to his parishioners for Christian life and action. Reading and reflecting on these pages gives us hope, deepens our faith and motivates us for Christian response. Fr Dasan says, 'It does not matter if our Christian charities are little or small. Little things are great to little people and great engines turn on small pivots.'

The paradoxical title, in a way, sums up our Christian vocation and life. You gain life when you lose it for Christ. Jesus emptied himself and God filled him with glory and power.

The Seasons of Grace invite us to thank and praise God. Fr Dasan's rflections end with prayers, which are a great help. As he says, 'God's power combined with our own Lenten sacrifices can transform the waters of chaos in our life into the wonders of creation.

I am sure that Fr Dasan's much pondered words will bring readers to truth out of falsehood, lead them to light from darkness and give them life in a civilisation of death.

Rev. Donatus Jeyaraj, S.J.
Jesuit Provincial, Tamilnadu province, India

Introduction

Were it not for the grace of God, there would be no such thing as a Christian. Grace is God's love that cures, stoops and rescues. Whatever is laudable in us proceeds from the grace of God. It reverts evil to innocence and the ancient to new. Man by nature is a wild horse dashing to the precipice, but, if grace is the Rider, he is restrained and turns away from danger. A little grace is better than many gifts. If I have one grain of grace, I must die to know how rich I am. Advent and Lent are special Seasons of grace.

Advent is the time for rousing. We are shaken to the very depths, so that we may wake up to the truth of ourselves. Advent grace helps us to let go of all our mistaken dreams, our conceited poses, arrogant gestures and all the pretences, so that Jesus who was born once according to the flesh may be born again in each of us according to the spirit. Beneath the predictable commotion of this season, we are able to catch the true sense of things, so ancient and so new, so intimate and so shattering .

We are all outside of paradise, locked up aboard an unsteerable ship, biding our time, unsure of ever reaching the land. But the Lent, which we observe amidst blood and sorrow, foreshadows our re-entering into paradise. The Lenten grace catches our ancient enemy like a fish, as it were by the hook of the cross, forcing him to eject those whom he has swallowed and to loose the booty which he held. The Lenten grace loosens the grip of evil and leads us, worn and weary by Lenten observance, to full and wholesome restoration.

But in order to avail ourselves of the lavishness of God's grace, one must approach the fountain of grace, conscious of his or her brokenness. One must feel deeply the need of grace. It is the economy of grace that emptying comes before filling, and poverty before forgiveness. Grace often grows strongest where conviction of sin has pierced deepest. Only the 'wounded deer leaps highest.' So too, only when we discover how wounded we are by our wayward lives with all the pain and darkness inside us, we will be able to jump and fall weeping in the arms of God, rejoicing in his forgiveness. Without the poverty of the spirit, there can be no abundance of grace.

This book contains reflections on the Scriptural Readings for all Sundays of Advent and Lent, covering all three years of the Liturgical Cycle. These were preached as homilies over three years at Sunday masses in Newmarket parish. Our people do not so much have to have their heads stored, as to have their hearts touched; but to touch people's hearts, a homily has to centre around the Word of God. A homily apart from the Word is a mistake in conception and a crime in execution. I hope that these reflections when preached touched the hearts of their listeners and will now touch their readers.

I thank the parishioners of the parish who gave acute and ardent attention fo these reflections when they were preached, and to many of them who prevailed on me to publish them. My deep felt thanks to Margaret Canning who had already printed these reflections in the Parish Newsletter even before they took their present shape. A distinct word of gratitude to my Jesuit Provincial for his thoughtful Foreword. Finally, I owe a large debt of gratitude to Stephen Dean, a man of few words but of many-layered competence, for coming forward to publish this book, and that in a delightful getup.

Vima Dasan, S.J.

CYCLE A

First Sunday of Advent, A

Isaiah 2:1-5; Romans 13:11-14; Matthew 24:37-44

Theme : We are called to meet Jesus as he comes daily into our lives, in order to prepare us for his final coming, when God's vision for mankind will become a reality.

MOST PEOPLE CAN SEE NO FARTHER THAN THEIR NOSES, but Isaiah read far into the mind of God and describes God's vision for the world (Is 2:1-5). A day will come, after the silence of ages and the long years of waiting, after all thrones have crumbled and crowns have fallen, when God will establish His Kingdom. In His kingdom 'all nations will stream towards the house of the Lord', for He will 'set all free to come out of isolation and form a family of nations.' All will take instructions from the Lord and walk in his path', for His instruction will be about justice, the great standing policy of His rule, and His path will be love, a love that can transform every human heart into a paradise on earth. Above all, in His reign, 'one nation will not raise the sword against another', for there will be no need for the blast of war - the unmitigated evil, planned by ambition, executed by violence and consummated by devastation. Peace will reign, the everlasting peace, never to be broken into pieces.

All people dream, and those who dream at night wake up only to find that it was vanity. But the dream of God for our world was not that it should fade into the light of common day, for it was not a Utopia, impractical and impossible of realisation.

Christ again and again spoke about 'the coming of the Son of Man' (Mt 24:37), and St Paul refers to it saying, 'our salvation is closer and the day draws near' (Rom.13:11). Therefore, we are certain beyond all doubt that one day the Lord will set up His rule, clothed in light and blinding the power of darkness, guiding all into the way of peace, drawing all to dwell in union of hearts and hands. But we do not know the exact day of His final coming. Any attempt to calculate the time of the end, a favourite preoccupation of many Christians, is doomed to failure; for it will be so sudden that 'when two men are at work, one will be taken, the other will be left' (Mt 24:40); that is, we will be caught up to meet Him with but a moment between here and there.

That will be His final coming. In the meantime, His reign has already begun. It began when Christ appeared, veiling his brightest glory, bearing our sins, dying on the cross and rising again. Christ himself had thus to inaugurate the reign of God, not only because it is he who will come at the end to reign as king, but also because only he can make nations into a Brotherhood, while science can only make them into a Neighbourhood. It is in order that we may appropriate more and more the fruits of Christ's death and resurrection and begin to taste even now the peace, love, truth and justice of his kingdom, that he keeps coming daily into our lives. He comes in the duties we carry out, in the things that happen to us and in the people we meet. His coming will be a surprise: 'The Son of Man is coming at the time you least expect' (Mt 24:44). This is true not only of his coming at the end of the ages and at the end of our lives, but also of his daily coming; hence the need for us to wait with minds and hearts always awake.

Visions are funny things; they never work unless you do. God's vision will soon become a reality, but only if we make His vision our own, by practising today the vision of tomorrow and by living the life of the kingdom here and now. This means we have to 'throw away our deeds of darkness', 'put on the armour of faith, hope and charity' (Rom 13:14), and work for peace and justice in the world. In international conflicts, tanks and missiles are deployed; in ethnic fights guns and bombs are fired; in community disputes knives and spears are wielded and in public life cruel actions and unjust deeds slash and cut each other. We need therefore to build bridges between people, by strengthening our relationships with one another, by taking initiatives to forgive, by loving the alienated and reaching out to the disadvantaged. Our work for the kingdom to come may be small and insignificant. But it is needed. As from little fountains large streams flow, and as from little acorns tall oaks grow, our little actions will mould the world to its glorious destiny, which is a promise from the Lord. It is this promise that makes every moment of our Christian life fly on wings of hope.

Let us pray.
Almighty God, give us grace, that we may cast away the works of darkness, and put upon the armour of light, now in this time of our mortal life, in which Thy Son Jesus came to visit us in great humility, that in the last day when he shall come again in his glorious majesty to judge both the living and the dead, we may rise to the life immortal.
Advent Sunday, Book of Common Prayer

2nd Sunday of Advent, A

A DAY WILL COME

Isaiah 11: 1–10; Romans 15:4-9; Matthew 3:1-12

Theme: Since a Day will definitely come when all people will be gathered together into one family as brothers and sisters, the Lord wants us to start living now in harmony with one another.

A DAY WILL COME WHEN JUSTICE WILL ROLL DOWN LIKE WATERS and righteousness like a mighty stream; for the king 'shall wear the band of justice around his waist'. A day will come when the loathsome mask of inequality will fall and all people will stand equal and undivided by class, so that even 'the wolf shall be the guest of the lamb'. A day will come, when there will be no enemies to fear but only friends to love; and even 'the baby shall play by the cobra's den', for 'there shall be no harm or ruin on the holy mountain of the Lord' (Is 11:5-9). On that day, all people, high and low, rich and poor, will sit together at the table of brotherhood and there will be neither east nor west, neither border nor breed, for the true nationality will be mankind. This is the picture of the kingdom, a return to the primeval harmony of Paradise, which Isaiah foresaw at the coming of Jesus Christ,.

Jesus Christ *did* come; but even now, in this world, might is master and justice is a servant, walking on wooden legs. Jesus Christ did come; but even now equality in many countries is a mortuary word; all men are born equal, yes, but eventually quite a few get over it. Christ did come, yes, but even so there is nothing commoner that the name 'friend', and nothing rarer than true friendship; some people spend their lives making enemies, others exterminating them. Christ did come, but many still keep asking 'Am I my brother's keeper?' A perverse idea of freedom; many indeed love their fellow human beings, but expect to make a living at it. As the human race draws nearer to the stars, we withdraw ourselves farther from our neighbour. So was Isaiah's vision just a fairy tale ? No. Christ did sow the seeds of the new kingdom and this kingdom is touching our lives even now, but it will fully come only in future, and we wait.

Our waiting has to be an active one. We have to prepare ourselves and the world to be ready to receive the new kingdom when it arrives. Since it will be a kingdom of justice, we must work *now* for justice for all, until justice forms the firm basis of all governments, not pity. Since in the new kingdom all will be equal, we must work now for equality for all, and not remain satisfied with the equality which begins only in the grave. Since harmony will be the soul of the holy music in the new kingdom, we must strive right now 'to live in perfect harmony with one another according to the spirit of Jesus' (Rom 15: 6). Since it will be a kingdom of friends, we must try right now to become to each other true friends in the Lord, not false friends, who roll out the carpet for you one day and pull it out from under you the next. Since in the new kingdom all will be brothers and sisters, we must right now come closer and closer to our neighbours. If all this demands that we reform our lives, we must do it, as St John the Baptist urges us to: 'Reform your lives for the kingdom of God is at hand' (Mt 3:2).

Such a time of waiting may be the hardest time of all. But only those who wait in this manner 'would mount up with wings as eagles' (Is 40: 3) towards the new kingdom which Isaiah saw in his vision. It was not a fairy story but the story of our salvation and hence it is our strong hope that such a kingdom will certainly come. To live without hope is the greatest human poverty, as you know. As a little child, having a bad nightmare, screams at night, we too, in the face of so much evil in the world, may get disheartened and frightened. But we need not. As the mother, hearing the child scream, runs to the bedroom, turns on the light and hugs the child saying, 'It's all right, don't worry; I'm here', so God comforts us saying, 'I am with you; your days may be weary, but I love you, you are mine'. So let us get to work. Advent offers us a rare opportunity to prepare for the coming of the Lord and his kingdom. Like the spoken word or the sped arrow, a neglected opportunity cannot come back.

Let us pray

Heavenly Father, we thank Thee for the vision of Thy purpose to gather all nations into a commonwealth of justice, love and brotherhood.

Forgive us for not seriously working for the fulfilment of your vision. The world is still racked by tensions and outright conflicts. Our goodwill towards men has no firm foundation, and crumbles at the first tremor of real testing.

Guide the leaders of nations into deeper unity and greater efforts for peace.

Turn to Thyself the hearts of all people, that by the power of the Holy Spirit, peace may be established

on the foundation of the values of Thy kingdom.

Hasten the time when justice and truth shall be established, and when all men shall be brought into one Family.

Stretch forth Thy hands in blessing over us Thy people, to heal our divisions, to restore us to peace and draw us to Thyself and to one another in love.

3rd Sunday of Advent, A

HE KEEPS COMING

Isaiah 35:1-6: James 5:7-10 Matthew 11:2-11

Theme: The Lord keeps coming to us in the midst of our daily toils and trials in order to lead us singing into everlasting joy.

WHERE GOD IS, THERE IS BEAUTY. We experience the beaming of his beauty in the flowering spring and in flowing rivers, on the fruitful plain and on the mountain heights, when the morning shines and when the birdlings sing. Where God is, there is joy; we experience it in the joy of love and hope, in the joy of peaceful conscience and of the grateful heart, in the joy of trustful soul and of glowing hope; we experience it even when 'the plants and trees rejoice and bloom with joyful song'(Is 35:1). Where God is, 'sorrows and mournings flee' (Is 35:10), for He heals the broken bodies and bruised hearts, with an overflow of the bright ocean of love. Just as torches burn most brightly when swung to and fro, so the healing presence of God brings out the rich qualities of a person, under the north wind of suffering. Where God is, the redemptive works of His Son Jesus continue. They were so profound and earth shattering that they continue to resonate thoughout the world even today, freeing men and women from bondage and darkness.

However, the mighty presence of God in the world does not yet banish the naughty presence of suffering from it. As long as we carry around our mortal bodies, wounded by sin, and until the Lord comes at the end of time, we must accept suffering willingly and even joyfully. We must permit no distress to break our friendship with God. A boy and girl are playing on the beach building sandcastles together, unaware of the approaching sea. Eventually the tide comes and sweeps their castle away. You know what they will do; they will laugh it off and walk hand in hand to another spot on the beach to build castles together again. Likewise, we may build castles real and unreal but God may wipe them out; at times we may feel that the landscape of our lives is turned into a desert, but even then we must hold on to God's hands and wait patiently for His coming, as 'the farmer awaits the precious field of his soil' (Jas 5:7), without 'murmuring or grumbling against one another' (v.9). Patience is not a beggar's virtue but the passion of great hearts.

The hearts of Christians must be great. If they are, they will not only bear their own sufferings willingly but also reach out to those who suffer, to lift their sorrows. Is it possible to list the ills of the present world that cry for help? Our dear world itself is sick for lack of basic elements: pure air, pure water and pure earth; for millions, life is like an onion which one peels in tears. Besides, it is our presence with those who suffer which makes us authentic Christians. Christ himself pointed out his ministry to the blind, lame, deaf and poor, as proof of his authenticity as Messiah (Mt 11:4). Hence a Christian heart has to go out offering help to those who are in distress; after all, our helping hand is just at the end of our own right arm. It does not matter if our charitable acts are only small. Little things are great to little people, and great engines turn on small pivots. Every small act of kindness extended to the afflicted, every act of charity we do to get justice for the poor, bread for the hungry and healing to the distressed, does bring God's liberating presence one step closer.

It is our unshakable belief that the presence of God in all its splendour will break out at the final coming of Christ, when 'all the ransomed will enter Zion singing, crowned with everlasting joy' (Is 35:10). But even before that day, Christ keeps coming to us here and now. Why? To open our eyes, if we are blind, to see the glory of God's presence in His creation and praise, and to see the misery of millions in our world and reach out; to open our ears, if we are deaf, to listen to God's word and obey, and to hear the cry of the poor and help; to strengthen our hands and knees, if they are feeble and weak to meet our commitments to God and our neighbour; to release our tongues, if we are dumb, to speak for justice and truth. Hence we must daily wait, especially during this Advent, for the Lord's visits. But not all his visits are announced; some of them come in disguise. So let us always keep awake for the Lord's visit; the mere opportunity to meet Him does not wake up those who are asleep.

Let us pray.
Lord, make me an instrument of your peace.
where there is hatred, let me sow love; where there is injury, pardon, where there is doubt, faith; where there is despair, hope; Where there is darkness, light; and where there is sadness, joy.
'Grant that I may not so much seek to be consoled as to console; to be understood as to understand; to be loved as to love;
for it is in giving that we receive; it is in pardoning that we are pardoned; and it is in dying that we are born to eternal life.

'Prayer of St. Francis'

4th Sunday of Advent - A

GOD IS WITH US

Isaiah 7:10-14; Romans 1:1-7; Matthew 1:18-24

Theme: We are preparing to celebrate the birth of Jesus, who is a God of puzzle and trouble, a God of presence and presents.

IF THERE IS ONE THING WHICH EVEN THE BEST GLUE CAN'T FIX, it is a broken promise. A broken pledge produces ever-widening ripples of distrust. In particular a promise made to a child, if not fulfilled, ruins confidence for ever. God our Father always keeps His promises, which are like life-preservers, keeping our souls from sinking into a sea of despair. God made a promise (Is 7:14) that 'a virgin shall be with a child and bear a son' who was to be the saviour of the world; and God did keep His word, by becoming man in the person of Jesus. But what sort of a God is our God, who came in flesh?

He is a God of PUZZLES. Not only did He surprise us by becoming man, but the way He came was still more surprising. 'Before Mary and Joseph lived together, she was found with a child through the power of the Holy Spirit' (Mt :18), with the result that Jesus was in the line of David in the human sphere, but Son of God in the divine; He is the God of the Jews as well as the God of the universe. We experience God's surprises in our own lives. Some of them are gentle shocks of mild surprise, others are giant tremors of big surprise. We ask for health that we might do greater things, but we are given infirmity that we might do better things; we ask for riches that we might be happy, but are given poverty that we might become wise; we ask for power that we may have the praise of men, but are given weakness that we may feel the need of God. So we must never give up on God in times of disappointments, for God has His surprises.

He is a God of TROUBLES. When He comes into our lives, trouble comes too. Christ's birth was meant to bring joy to Mary and Joseph, but what an agony of mind Joseph had to wrestle with when he found his wife pregnant. This is true in our lives also. Our commitment to God, church and neighbour, brings with it slings and arrows of sometimes outrageous troubles. If we are poor we suffer from want of money, but if we are rich we suffer from troubles which money can't cure. Marriage vows are meant to bring joy, but often they bring sorrow; sex is meant for faithful love but at times it brings on intolerable pregnancies. But we know for sure that when we have troubles, God comes. He came to Joseph to assure him saying, 'Have no fear about taking Mary as your wife' (Mt 1: 20) and He gave him reasons too. So when we are in trouble let us trust that God is closest to us and will bring some good out of our troubles. As soft marrow abides in hard bones, blessings abide in troubles. Troubles are often tools by which God fashions us for better things. Anyway, what is the use of worrying? Better to pack up our troubles in an old kitbag and take it to the Lord.

He is a God of PRESENCE. When God became man, human nature was raised to a divine dignity; the Son of God has united himself in some fashion with every human; everything material has received a spark of the spiritual; all creation has been illuminated by his divine light; God has fixed His abode here on earth. Hence, 'they shall call him Emmanuel, a name which means 'God is with us' (Mt 1:23). If we know how to look around for God, we can see Him smiling and hear Him speaking, even in the smallest and most ordinary events in our lives. I picked up the phone and talked to a friend but he hung up suddenly. I was hurt, but God smiled at me and said, 'You talked a lot and listened very little. Since you didn't listen, you learned nothing, helped nothing, and communicated nothing. Stop this monologue and you will have friends'. God is present in Christian community; 'where two or three are gathered in my name, I am there' (Mt 18:20). We can see God's goodness in the kindness of others and experience His happiness in our own joy and peace. He is there in our illness comforting us; He is in our celebrations like Christmas, bringing families together in love.

He is a God of PRESENTS. His presence may be ordinary but His presents are extraordinary. He gives 'salvation from sins' (Is 1 :23); He gives 'holiness, grace and peace' (Rom 1:7). God is with us in moments of sorrow, giving solace; in situations of poverty, giving support and in times of worry, giving peace. He is with us to see through any struggle and to strengthen us to endure any disappointments. Christmas is a time to reaffirm our faith, that 'God is with us' and 'will be with us' to the end of time.

Lord Jesus Christ, you are Lord of surprises.

You came to a stable when men looked in a palace, You were born in poverty when we might have expected riches; King of all the earth you were content to visit one nation. From beginning to end you upturned our human values and held us in suspense.

Come to us, Lord Jesus. Do not let us take you for granted, or pretend that we ever fully understand you. Continue to surprise us, so that kept alert, we are always ready to receive you as Lord and to do your will'
Donald Hilton, b.1932

20

Christmas Day: a first look

DAWN ON OUR DARKNESS

!saiah 52:7-10; Hebrews 1:1-6; John 1:1-18

Theme: Christ came into the world as the dawn on our darkness, so that anyone who believes in him and receives him into his life as his Saviour, is in the light.

NO ONE IS LIGHT UNTO HIMSELF, NOT EVEN THE SUN. Christ alone is the Light. Before his birth, people were in darkness, confused about the very meaning of life, and like infants were crying for light, with no language but a cry. But God sent His light and brilliancy in Christ, before the jaws of death could devour us. Viktor Frankl was a Nazi prisoner in World War II. One early morning he and some other prisioners were digging in the cold hard ground. As he was struggling to find a reason for all his sufferings and slow dying, suddenly he became totally convinced that there was a reason, though he could not fully understand it. He writes in his book *Man's Search For Meaning*: 'At that moment a Light was lit in the distant farm house which stood on the horizon, as if it were painted there in the midst of the miserable grey'. At that moment, he says that the words of the gospel flashed into his mind: 'The light shines in the darkness and the darkness has never put it out' (Jn 1:5). From then, Victor was a different man, for it gave him hope and dispelled his despair.

There are times in our lives when we are thrown into

darkness, in which even shameful deeds do not bring disgrace; but if we open our hearts to Christ, he can dispel our darkness. When we do something wrong and try to hide it, our deeds are in the dark; but the light of Christ can reveal our deeds as they are, moving us to acknowledge our guilt and repent. When we don't know what to do or what to say, our minds are in the dark; but his light can remove that ignorance, urging us to help those who are afraid to speak on behalf of the poor. When we don't see any purpose in life, our life is in the dark; but his light can help us to find meaning in our life. When we can't accept Jesus into our lives as our Saviour, our life is in the dark; but his light can offer us the gift of faith, if we truly open our hearts to him. When we fear death, because we don't hope for anything beyond the grave, our death is in the dark; but his light can reveal him as our resurrection. Hence, when our light is low and the quiet shadows are falling, when our blood creeps, the nerves prick and the heart is sick, we must seek the light of Christ.

So many centuries have gone by since the coming of Christ and yet, perhaps, we are still in the dark. How do we know that it is day and that for a Christian the night is over? Is it, when in the morning, we can distinguish a mango tree from an apple tree, or an ox from an ass? Not really. When we look at our neighbour and recognize, in him or her, our own brother or sister, then it is day for us, then we are in the light of Christ; for love of neighbour is the heart of Christ's message. As long as this is not the case, we are still in darkness, which Christ alone can remove, for he is the brightest and best of the sons of the morning, streaming light on our darkness. Hence we cannot remove our darkness all by himself; we have to first open our hearts to him. A famous artist drew a magnificent picture of Christ, thorn crowned, and carrying a lantern in his left hand, knocking at a closed door. He entitled the picture *The Light Of The World*. A friend of his who greatly appreciated the painting said to him: 'But you have put no handle on the door!' The artist replied, 'You forgot, the handle is on the inside'.

Likewise Jesus is willing to fill us with his light, as sunlight is willing to flood a room that is open to its brightness, but we must open our hearts to the light, for we have the key. Once filled with his light, we can become light to others. As children of the light, we are called to become a beam of light in the midst of darkness and a ray of hope in the midst of despair. It is not enough to decorate our homes and trees with Christmas lights. We ourselves must become lights, and light candles from our own light instead of cursing the darkness. We are called to shed Christ's light on others by our example; example is always more efficacious than precepts, for precept begins, example accomplishes. Our example must be a witness to our religious faith, in the midst of a world that often ridicules religious faith as superstition; a witness to human dignity, in the midst of a world that often tramples on human rights.

May we become bearers of the light to help people out of darkness and shadows of death, and thus leave a trail of Christ-light behind us as we pass through this life.

Let us pray.
Lead, kindly light, amid the encircling gloom;
lead thou me on :
the night is dark and I am far from home;
lead thou me on.
Keep thou my feet; I do not ask to see
the distant scene; one step enough for me.

John Henry Newman

1st Sunday of Lent - A

LENT IS IDEAL

Genesis 2:7-9, 3:1-7; Romans 5:12-19; Matthew 4:1-11

Theme: Lent offers us an ideal opportunity to renew our lives, by taking decisions based on the Word of God, and aided by the Grace of God operative in Christ

FRIENDSHIP WILL LAST IF YOU PUT IT FIRST. But Adam and Eve did not. In their ill-woven ambition, hunting impossibilities on the wings of hope to reverse roles with their Creator and Friend, they ate the fruit forbidden by Him (Gen.3.6) and lost His friendship. Their friendship with God was like sound health, the value of which they did not know until it was lost, because their rejection of God's Word brought with it also the collapse of their harmonious relationship with their fellow human beings and Nature, introducing evil, suffering and eco-logical devastation into the world (Gen. 3:7). But God's love has a hem to its garment, that reaches the very dust touching the stains of the streets and lanes. In His love God sent His Son Jesus to restore humanity's friendship with God, which Jesus accom-plished by his self-sacrifice. However, curses are like young chickens: they come home to roost. So the curse suffered by our first parents began haunting human nature, with the result that everyone carries within their mortal frame a proclivity to reject God so that they can be God to themselves, a fatal and perfidious ambition which first sprang from the blessed abode.

We commit only the oldest sin but in the newest kind of

ways. Beneath the dingy uniformity of international fashions in dress, we are always the same, capable of outstanding courage and open to outrageous temptations. We are tempted to substitute our own ways for God's ways; to use other people's and one's own gifts for totally selfish purposes; and to misuse our position, talent and wealth for our own vaulting ambition. The temptation to cater for excessive bodily comforts, without any self-denial; the readiness to substitute decent principles which are for all ages, with expedients which are for the hour, and to substitute the superficial for the real, the trivial for the tremendous: these are temptations to a false way of life. Falsehood is the jockey of misfortune, and hence Jesus warned us about all of these. He also gave us an example of how to fight temptation, since example is the lesson we can all read. In the desert he was tempted (Is.4:1-11) to compromise his mission by substituting self-interest for God's interest, the values of the world for the ways of God, the immediate and attractive realities for the will of God; but he rejected all of them, relying only on God's Word.

But we must be right about this. God never overpowers anyone with temptations, but allows them only to test our faithfulness to Him. Temptations are suggestions for us either to reject or accept God's friendship. The pity is that some take evil suggestions as a cat laps milk; others start playing with them. How can you play with the animal in you, without becoming wholly animal? How can you keep your garden tidy, while reserving a plot for weeds? We must resist evil at its mere suggestion. It is better to shun the bait than struggle in the snare. In every temptation we are called to make a personal decision either for God or against Him, with a concern also for the social implications of our decision. For when I sin, there is so much more evil in the world, but when I respond to grace, there is so much more good. To help us choose God in our decisions the grace of God is always available in Christ, 'for if by offence of one man all die, much more did the gracious gift of the one man Christ, abound for all' (Rom. 5:17).

Lent is the right time to take right decisions. On this desert journey towards Easter, the word of God will challenge us to choose Him and His ways above all else, aided by the gracious activity of God in Christ. If we have to change our attitudes towards God, our fellow men and Nature around us, we must change. Change is only the interval between the decay of the old and formation of the new. We can't be like wood, which may lie ten years in the water but will never become a crocodile. To bring about the desired changes in our lives during Lent we are advised to go into 'desert' as often as we can, like Jesus. Deserts are like stars but with a difference: stars speak of our insignificance in the long eternity of time, whereas deserts speak of our insignificance right now. Our 'desert' can be any private moment in a private place, stripped of all the world's distractions and attractions. Jesus was careful to use the right weapons to combat evil: prayer, penance and the Word of God; so must we. Weapons must be as strong as the enemy; one can't shoot with butter but with guns.

> Let us pray.
> O Lord, you marked us with the sign of mortality,
> the dust of last year's palm;
> but the cross you traced on our furrowed brows has not turned us from sin.
> Because we have sinned, our human nature, created in your image,
> has become shapeless, uncomely, and ready to be laid in the grave.
> But we are prepared to begin our spiritual combat again.
> Grant us that this day be a day of new beginnings,
>   a time to remember your grace and move on;
>   your mighty grace can make for us a world of difference,
> as faith and hope are born again by the life and death of Jesus your Son.

26

2nd Sunday of Lent - A

THE IMMORTAL DIAMOND

Genesis 12:1-4; 2 Tim 1.8-10; Matthew 17:1-9

Theme: We Christians baptized in Christ, live in the hope that one day our ordinary humanity will be transformed like the transfigured Christ, into new being, radiant as an immortal diamond.

IT IS A BURDEN TO SOME OF US TO BE HUMAN BEINGS, to some others it is shame and disgrace to carry around a human body; still others ride through life as if on a beast within. But the Transfiguration of Christ is a demonstration of what our human nature is destined for, and what our humanity is capable of. Our life may be a moment, less than a moment, but a moment will come, when in a flash and at a trumpet crash, we will all at once be transfigured into what Christ was on Mount Tabor, 'dazzling as the sun and radiant as light' (Mt.17:2). Our humanity may be debased by slavery, corrupted by power or degraded into a mass of animated dust, but the light of God which it conceals will finally break through. Yes, the fall of a leaf is a whisper to every living creature that mankind are earthen jugs; but the marvel is, that it carries within an immortal diamond.

The feast of the Transfiguration is a feast of encouragement. One day the devil decided to put a few of his well-worn tools up for sale. On display were some treacherous instruments including hatred, jealousy, lying and pride. Set apart from the rest, however, was a harmless-looking device with a very high price tag. 'What's that?' someone asked. 'That's discouragement,' Satan replied, 'it is one of my most effective tools; with it I pry open the hearts of God's greatest servants and bring on depression.' Hence, when we are in trouble, we must take care not to fall into the devil's snare. Trouble has no necessary connection with discouragement. As arthritis is different from stiff joints, so trouble is different from discouragement, which has a germ of its own. If we are discouraged, we would soon slide into despair; and there is no vulture like despair. On the contrary, we are encouraged by the Lord's Transfiguration to persist and persevere in the midst of troubles, for it radiates hope in the ultimate victory of the good. 'Listen, to my beloved Son,' says the heavenly Father; and Jesus says, 'Rise and have no fear'.

The glory promised by Christ's Transfiguration, at which humanity will finally arrive, is already possessed by us through baptism. This means that an enormous vitality and dignity lie concealed in ordinary humanity; and it has indeed burst forth with all its power in many great figures in the history of the church's social mission, who have always been pioneers in education, health-care and social change. Christians who believe that they possess an immortal diamond of glory will cease to be pessimists, always expecting the worst and making the worst of it when it happens. Rather, they will soon learn in their Christian journey that even in the midst of winter there is in them an invincible summer, always aware that 'Christ has robbed death of its power and has brought life and immortality' (1 Tim.1:10). Such Christian optimists will smile through trials and tribulations, for they know that what sunshine is to flowers, smiles are to humanity.

We may find our lives filled with trifles, to be sure; but scattered along life's pathways, the good even trifles can do is immeasurable. However, to grasp the significance of small things around us and sundry events in our lives, one has to be awake. 'They kept awake and saw His glory' (Lk.9:32). If our minds are not asleep, we will lose much in life. Prior to our final glory, we will have our imperfect transfigurations, for example in prayer, which could be a moment of grace to become more loving and alive to God. Even outside prayer, we will have our moments of happiness, for example, when we go for a walk after a tiring day or when we re-establish friendship after a quarrel. But once again, in order to experience God at such moments one has to be awake. A woman at a bank asked the cashier to cash a cheque for her. Citing company policy, the cashier asked for her identification. The woman gasped. Finally she managed to say, 'But, Jonathan, I'm your mother!' So, let us be awake.

Let us pray.

0 God, who before the Passion of thy only-begotten Son didst reveal his glory upon the holy mountain, grant unto us thy servants, that in faith beholding the light of his countenance, we may be strengthened to bear the cross, and be changed into his likeness from glory to glory, through the same Jesus Christ our Lord.

Feast of the Transfiguration, Book of Common Prayer

3rd Sunday of Lent, A

THE LIVING WATER

Exodus 17:3-7; Romans 5:1-8; John 4:5-42

Theme: Christ offers Living Water, the very life of God, to satisfy the deep-down thirst of the human heart.

ALL OVER THE WORLD COMPANIES LIKE COCA-COLA AND PEPSI spend millions on TV ads, intended to whet our thirst for a drink. But most people, today, thirst for things of greater value. They thirst for justice, truth and love; they long for recognition, freedom and security, like the Samaritan woman of the gospel, who, oppressed by the prejudice and injustice of a foreign power and crushed by her own guilty conscience was herself seeking after freedom and peace. But the tragedy is that many try to satisfy this inner craving of the human heart with material things. Material things can never fill our inner void, for ours is a spiritual thirst, basically a thirst for God. St Augustine rightly said, 'Our hearts are made for God and they will not rest until they rest in God'. Trying to satisfy our thirst for God with material things is like trying to distract a crying baby by giving it candy and by making funny faces at it. Material pleasures are like the snowball in the river, white for a moment , then melting for ever, leaving us thirsting for things of greater value.

But God has provided us a way to satisfy our inner thirst. He has given us Living Water through His Son Jesus Christ. Jesus said, 'Whoever drinks the water I give will never be thirsty'

(Jn.4.14). The Living Water that Christ gives is the life of God Himself. Since God is Love, it is the very 'love of God that was poured into our hearts' (Rom.5:5) at our baptism. It is for this love of God flowing from His Holy Spirit that we actually thirst, as people in parched lands thirst for water. It originated from the pierced side of Christ on the cross and continues to flow into the bloodstream of the Church whose members we are. It gives divine life to our souls now and immortality to our bodies at resurrection. It frees us from clinging to material things, from clinging to unforgiving ancient hatreds, and from clinging to sinful pleasures. Since the living water is the life of God who is Love itself, we should immerse our hearts, with all the holes in them, into the ocean of God's love. Once immersed in water, what does it matter whether our human heart has holes or not?

Where can we find this Living Water? It is in Christ. He is the Rock. As Moses struck the rock in the desert and water gushed forth (Ex.17.6), so when Christ was pierced with a lance, the living water flowed and still flows. As Christ was present to the Samaritan woman in her search for peace, which even five husbands could not give, so he is present in our search for peace and in the midst of our painful existence; so painful, that after having gone to several wells, wells of power, of prestige, of success, of money and of pleasures, we still remain unsatisfied. Christ is present in his words and in the Sacraments. By experiencing Christ personally in prayer we can receive the water of peace; by following him we can drink the water of freedom; and by serving his people we can receive the water of joy. None of us need, therefore, ask like the Israelites, 'Is the Lord in our midst or not?' (Ex 17:7). But the pity is that some of us seem to be hardly aware of his presence, as people who go through a forest but find no firewood. A greater poverty than that caused by lack of money is the poverty of unawareness.

God's life that flows into us through Christ, is not to be smothered or hidden away. It is not water to be stored in a tank. It is given to be shared. That is why, in those who drink from it, it 'becomes a fountain 'within them,leaping up to provide eternal life' (Jn.4:14). Are we prepared like the Samaritan woman, to share this water of life with so many others who are in need of it, peoples such as those who live in blindness, in abject poverty, in wheel- chairs, in sickness and in thousands of other harsh and hostile situations? Even the strong, rich and powerful will need it, for riches may fill your pockets but it usually leaves the hearts empty. Lenten prayers, fastings and good works offer us a precious opportunity to drink this life-giving Water to the full and share it with others as well. Lenten liturgy brings us closer than ever to the fountain of the living water. But let not the liturgy distract us from the life it brings, for the bucket is not the thing, but the water it contains.

> *Let us pray.*
> *God of power*
> *you sent your Son to be our Saviour.*
> *Grant that we, who, like the woman of Samaria, thirst for living water,*
> *may turn to the Lord as we hear God's word*
> *and acknowledge our sins and weaknesses that weigh us down.*
> *Protect us from vain reliance on self*
> *and defend us from the power of Satan.*
> *Free us from the spirit of deceit,*
> *so that, admitting the wrong we have done,*
> *we may attain purity of heart and advance on the way to salvation*
>
> *Rite of Christian Initiation of Adults: First Scrutiny (slightly adapted)*

4th Sunday of Lent - A

OUT OF DARKNESS

1 Samuel 16:1-3; Ephesians 5:8-14; John 5:1-41

Theme: In baptism we were delivered from darkness, so that we may walk in the light of the risen Lord.

THE JOY OF SEEING FOR THE FIRST TIME IS UNSPEAKABLE. During World War II, John Howard was blinded in an aeroplane explosion and could not see a thing for the next twelve years. But one day as he was walking down a street near his parents' home in Texas, suddenly he began to see 'red sand' in front of his eyes. Without warning his sight returned again. According to an eye specialist, a blocking of blood to the optic nerve, caused by the explosion, had cleared. Commenting on this experience John said, 'You don't know what it is for a father to see his children for the first time'. But according to the gospel (Jn.9:7), something more spectacular happened to a man born blind, for Christ conferred on him, not only his physical sight but also spiritual sight; He opened his inner eyes of faith, and radiated His own light into the mind and heart of the blind man, so that, the blind man believed in Jesus, as one believes in the sun.

We too received the same gift of faith at our baptism: a faith without which there is neither hope nor love, for it alone grasps meaning in the midst of meaninglessness; a faith that sings like a bird, while the dawn is still dark, for it can turn away any curse, light any path, relieve any distress, bring joy out of sorrow and heaven out of hell. At baptism we too received the light of Christ, a light for which restless millions waited for ages, whose dawn makes all things new; a light that gives more than sight, for it enables us to emerge from the tombs of sin and death into the day light of Christ's life. 'There was a time when you were in darkness but now you are light in the Lord' (Eph.5:8). That time was before our baptism. We were all blind and in the dark, until we came to see in faith who Jesus really is and what is the light he has to offer us. Similar to the anointing of David (I Sam. 16.13) and the smearing of the blind man's eyes (Jn.9:6), we too received anointing in the sacrament of baptism, a sign of God's call to live and witness to the life of the children of the light.

We are the children of the light if our hearts are pleasing to God, however low or lofty our stature. In the world people are valued not for what they are but what they seem to be. But God chose David as King, in spite of his shabby appearance, because he was a man after His own heart (Sam.16:12). We are the children of the light not because we are able to distinguish, in daylight, an ox from an ass but because we can recognize in our neighbours our own brothers and sisters. We are the children of the light if we 'produce every kind of goodness, justice and truth' (Eph 5:9) and commit ourselves to these values with courage, a courage that is grace under pressure. We are the children of the light if we live as true Christians in the world, unstained by its evil, like Christ's own light which can pass through pollution without being polluted. We are the children of the light, if, enlightened by the beam of Christ's brightness and bearing in our hands the light that shines for all, we bring light to those whose eyes cannot see, because their hearts wish them to be blind.

Lent is the time for each of us to ask whether we are in the light or still in the dark. Do we overlook people in need and keep discussing only the abstract question of evil in the world, like the disciples, who asked whose fault it was that the man was blind? Are we blind and perhaps glory in being blind - the very limit of human blindness - to the sufferings of the poor and the sick, the oppressed and the abandoned? Are we afraid to support just causes like the parents of the blind man, who would not stand up for him out of fear of authorities? Our fears always outnumber our dangers! Is our faith weak to see any good beyond our sorrows? The heart of a Christian is like a creeping plant which withers, for want of faith, which it needs to entwine. Are we blind to our own faults which are not in the stars but in ourselves? In order not to face them, do we always blame others? The greatest of faults is to be conscious of none. The time is drawing near for the renewal of our baptismal promises in the Holy Saturday liturgy. May we therefore come out of darkness and begin walking in the light of the risen Lord.

Let us pray.
Lord Jesus,
you are the true light that enlightens the world.
Through your Spirit of truth
protect us from being enslaved by the father of lies.
Stir up in us the desire for good.
Let us rejoice in your light, that we may see,
and, like the man born blind whose sight you restored,
let us prove to be staunch and fearless witnesses to the faith,
for you are Lord for ever and ever.

Rite of Christian Initiation of Adults

5th Sunday of Lent - A

BEGIN HERE AND NOW

Ezodus 37:12-14; Romans 8:8-11; John 11:1-45

Theme: Anyone who is united to Christ through belief in Him begins eternal life, here and now.

EVEN AT OUR BIRTH, DEATH DOES BUT STAND ASIDE A LITTLE. It eats up everything, both the young lamb and the old sheep. People die of cancer, old age, car accidents, war, starvation and disease. But for Christians, death is the supreme festival on the road to eternal life. We believe with the prophet Ezekiel that out of the graves new life will emerge (Ez.37:12); with St Paul we trust 'that God who raised Jesus from the dead will raise us also to new life' (Rom.8:11); because the Lord said that those who believe in him, 'though they should die, will come to life' (Jn.11:25). Eternal life is not something that only comes after our physical death; it can begin here and now, in and through any of the kinds of living death that we face. Breakdown in marriage, unemployment, becoming a victim of crime and violence, bereavement, anxiety, self-doubt and guilt, may well be an experience of death that takes us piecemeal, not at a gulp. But however devastating these deaths may be, those who make a leap of faith in the midst of such disillusionment will find eternal life here and now; for the Lord said, not 'I *will be*' but 'I *am* the resurrection and the life' (Jn.11:25).

But to experience eternal life here and now one must believe in Christ, precisely because faith unites us to him, and he is that life. The raising of Lazarus was not meant just to console his sisters, but to serve as the symbol of the presence of eternal life in the person who believes in Christ. This life of faith is not some vague affirmation about Christ. It is living with Jesus' Spirit. 'If anyone does not have the Spirit of Christ, he does not belong to him' (Rom.5.9). It calls us to a behaviour, which is inspired by Christ's own behaviour. It is unselfish life. It consists in dying to oneself, which is living for God and others. It is giving our time, our resources, our energy and ourselves in the service of our neighbour. As a little child who already possesses the power to grow into manhood or womanhood, we Christians through our baptism already possess the power to live an unselfish life. Has this power grown in us, given us deeper and deeper experience of the new life in Christ? If not, we are called to begin a spiritual return, as the Israelites returned from the exile to their homeland. If we still find ourselves in the tomb of selfishness, we are called to come out of the tomb, as Lazarus came out. Our selfishness makes us hard and stiff towards others. Hardness and stiffness are companions of death, not of life. Look at a man at his birth; he is tender and supple, but at death he is hard and stiff! Therefore, we need conversion, constant conversion, from the sinfulness of the 'flesh' and the 'self' to the new life of the Spirit and love. Of course any change for the better would cause pain and suffering. But, it is only from human emptiness that a person can find the fullness of God. Only from darkness comes the dawn. In the sunlight of happy days, faith may be golden; but it is in the midst of sadness and suffering that we are called to take the leap of faith. It is in the moment of human darkness that we are called to believe in our immortal destiny, beyond death.

Lent is nearing its end. God calls us again to change. If we feel we are too settled to change, if we fear we have been too long in the grave of mediocrity, God can help us with His power. Lazarus came to life not by his own power, but by the power of God. It is the power of God that enables us to break out of the fetters of fear-filled self-centredness. Therefore, we must bring all our fears and frailties to God in prayer. Martha brought her sadness to the Lord and her sadness was transformed into a faith-experience that her brother was not dead but alive with God. So, instead of living in self-imposed Friday darkness, let us bring our deepest fears and deadly darkness to God in prayer. God's power, combined with our own Lenten sacrifices, can transform the waters of chaos in our life into the wonders of creation.

Let us pray.
Lord Jesus, before your death you raised Lazarus from the dead and shook the dominion of death.

Through him whom you loved, you have foretold the deliverance of all from corruption and showed that you came that we might have life, and have it more abundantly.

Free us from the grasp of death and deliver us from the corruption of sin.

Passion Sunday, A

AGONY AND GLORY

Isaiah 50.4–7; Phillippians 2:6 –11; Matthew 26:14–27:66

Theme: Those who suffer like Christ for the love of God and neighbour, may hit the rock bottom of agony, but are sure to rise to the height of glory.

OUR LORD JESUS SUFFERED AND DIED FOR LOVE OF GOD AND MAN; and the fact that all through His passion He suffered alone brings out the depth of His love, for loneliness is the clearest indication of a person's capacity to love. The fact that He suffered, not because of weaknesses inherent in human nature, but as the result of human injustice and of his revolutionary message, proves His faithful love for God and man. In His suffering He acted upon his own words: 'The greatest love a person can have for his friends, is to give his life for them' (Jn.15:13). Our Lord did not suffer to wipe out sufferings from our lives, but to teach us how to suffer, to teach us that suffering will always accompany true love; and hence anyone who follows him must carry his daily cross (Mt.18:34). He taught us about the supremacy of love and of the qualities that exemplify it, namely that love is stronger than violence, that humility is stronger than pride, that kindness is stronger than anger, that gentleness is stronger than rudeness and that peace is stronger than war.

The apparent futility of suffering runs through the whole of

Christ's passion. His mission seems to be about to end in failure. But He overcomes the apparent futility by abiding obedience to his Father's will. 'He humbled himself, obediently accepting even death, death on the cross' (Phil.2:8); and He did so freely. He gave his back to those who beat him' (Is.50:6), being fully in control of his destiny, whereas, others during the passion acted as prisoners. Pilate was utterly imprisoned by his own weakness; the high priests were contolled not by truth but by their lust for the blood of Jesus. Peter could not control even his tongue and denied his master; Judas ended his life as a prisoner of his own hopelessness. But Jesus was all the time free, so free that He would later say, 'I am now ready for you'. It is this freedom with which Christ chose to suffer for the love of us, adds crown to His passion. Of course He needed help, which He could not expect from His own disciples, who slept when He suffered and woke up only to desert Him. Christ's constant prayer was, 'The Lord God is my help' (Is.50:7).

Like Christ, those who love God and neighbour, must be ready to face conflicts, sufferings and even death. In the past many have laid down their lives for the sake of love. There are thousands who are presently imprisoned unjustly for their Christian convictions. To try to face each day, like a true Christian with courage, in a world which requires so many kinds of pain-killers, can be very hard. Struggle for social justice and human freedom will involve some forms of death: death to one's position, honour, wealth and power, sometimes even physical death. But if our love of God and neighbour is deep and strong, we will be able to accept these sufferings freely, as a way of sharing in Christ's love. We would also be able in love to reach out to others and diminish their sufferings. We would be able to see in those who suffer the face of the contemporary Christ, marred and scarred by the violence which human beings inflict upon each other, without being silent; for such a silence would only inflict further violence, of neglect and carelessness, on those who suffer.

Victory comes through suffering. Passion was not the last word in the life of Christ. It was only the first word of the Holy Week, that will reach its climax on Easter Sunday. So too, no matter how many of our days seem to end in a depressing way, they are not the last word in our life. Rather they are only the prelude to triumphs we have yet to experience in this life, and they point to the ultimate victory, which will be ours in the next life. Hitting rock bottom in our personal life and falling into the depth of sin must not make us pessimistic. No matter how low we fall, there is always the possibility of rising from it to the height.

Palm Sunday should solidify our hope. Palms should be signs that we are willing to march with Jesus, not only in moments of triumphs and glory, but also in times of suffering and agony. For the passion and the resurrection of Jesus prove that life will prevail over death, that when death has done even its worst, life will win over.

Let us pray.
Almighty God, your most dear Son went not up to joy but first he suffered pain, and entered not into glory before he was crucified. Mercifully grant that we, walking in the way of the cross, may find it none other than the way of life and peace. We ask this through the same Jesus Christ.

Book Of Common Prayer

CYCLE B

First Sunday of Advent, B

WAITING FOR THE LORD

Isaiah 63:16–17,19; 64:2–7; I Cor 1 :3–9; Mk 13:33–37

Theme :If only we have those eyes that see and those ears that hea,r Christmas can be a pointer to the constant coming of Christ in our lives.

ONCE I WENT TO SEE MY PARENTS, AFTER A LONG ABSENCE. My mother lovingly scolded me saying, 'Do you know how long we have been waiting for you?' I said, 'I understand, mother, but do you know how long I was waiting to be born?' All of us wait to be born, to be nourished and to be loved. Travellers wait for buses and planes; students wait for the results of their exams. Waiting is part of life. Life is not like instant coffee, there is always more to life than we can grasp its fulness at any one time. If it is so with life of man, what of the life of God, whose glory shines not in one sun but in numberless suns and whose greatness flashes not in one world but in ten hundred thousands of infinite globes? When we see the stars and hear the mighty thunder, his power throughout the universe displayed, can we ever imagine, that we can at any one time grasp the immensity of God! Can we ever fathom the depth of God's love, 'who so loved us that He gave His only begotten Son'? We say 'God is love', but can we at any given moment possess all His love, which is the same in days of calm or in days of storm and which is deeper than our sorrows, deeper than our death and deeper than our sins? Even to write of God's love would drain the ocean dry. Hence all that we can do is to wait for God to let Himself be known and be possessed as He pleases.

Advent calls us to wait for the Lord. Today's liturgy under-lines this waiting. Isaiah expresses our intense desire as we wait for the Lord: 'Oh, that you would rend the heavens and come down' (Is 64:1). St Paul assures the Corinthians that they 'lack no spiritual gifts as they wait for the revelation of our Lord Jesus' (1 Cor 1:7). Jesus in the Gospel asks us 'to be awake and vigilant' (Mk 13: 33). Surely we must wait for the Lord who will come at the moment of our death. Death is no respecter of persons, but lays his icy hands even on kings, as their sceptre and crown crumble away. You cannot take a newspaper without finding that death has a corner in it. Hence Advent calls us always to be ready to meet the Lord at our death. But as Christians, we should be ready not just for the final coming of Christ but for his constant coming every day of our lives.

If we are alert, we can find the Lord popping up in the ordinary activities and possibilities of life. If I am watchful, he may be tapping me on my shoulder when I meet my neighbour. If only we have 'those eyes that see, those ears that hear' (Is 64:4), we can meet him in his supreme visit. which he makes in a thousand ways. If we look wide-eyed at all creation, which reflects God, when the flowers of the earth are springing, the birds of the sky singing and a world of blended beauties smiling; we can sense through the sacred feelings they arouse in us the rustling of His garments and the coming of His feet. Even when the wintry winds are howling and the heavens darkly scowling, we can feel the awesome majesty of His giant steps. Yes, to meet the Lord, we must be prepared for life, not just for death.

Advent is the countdown time for the celebration of Christmas. But Christmas is only a pointer to the constant coming of Christ in our lives. When we do Christmas shopping and buy gifts rightly suited to each friend, Jesus comes in the respect we show to the uniqueness of each individual; when we send Christmas cards with messages of love, Jesus comes through the warmth and affection we express to others; when we decorate our homes and streets, Jesus comes through our desire to bring beauty into other people's lives; when we prepare our Christmas family meal, Jesus comes through our readiness to make peace with all and form one human family. The Lord is willing to come as light is willing to flood a room but we have to wait for him with our minds and hearts open and vigilant. God's love is pressing round us on all sides like air.

Let us pray.
Lord God, we adore you because you have come to us in the past; you have spoken to us in the Law of Israel;
you have challenged us in the words of the Prophets; you have shown us in Jesus what you are really like.
Lord God, we adore you because you still come to us now;
you come to us through other people and their loving concern for us you come to us through men and women who need our help; : you come to us as we worship you with your people.
Lord God, we adore you because you will come to us at the end;
you will be with us at the hour of death;
you will still reign supreme, when all human institutions fail;.
you will still be God when our history has run its course.
we welcome you, the God who comes.
Come to us now in the power of Jesus Christ our Lord.

Anon.

2nd Sunday of Advent, B

HE IS HERE

Isaiah 40:1-5, 9-11; II Peter 3: 8-14; Mark 1:1-8

Theme: During Advent we need to get into a symbolic desert experience in order to experience God who is already here.

LIFE IS LIKE HEADY WINE. EVERY ONE READS THE LABEL ON THE bottle, but hardly any one tastes the wine. That is why there is such a craving in each of us for better life. The search for better life goes on, but often, in the wrong places. Here is an Indian story: A neighbour found Nasuruddin on hands and knees. 'what are you searching for, Mullah?' 'My key.' Both men got on their knees to search. After a while the neighbour says, 'Where did you lose it?' 'At home.' 'Good Lord. Then why are you searching here?' 'Because it's brighter here!' We must search for better life where we lost it and we lost it where God is; and where God is, there is 'New Heaven and New Earth' (II Pet 3:13).

When shall we enter into this New Heaven and New Earth? Is it only after death? No. God is present here and now. When the Lord was made flesh, God in the person of Jesus literally entered into this material world, into a human body, experiencing all the sufferings and death we do but dramatically rising again from the dead. So this God is with us, in the midst of our sins and sufferings, giving us an experience of His presence and raising us to better life, as He raised His Son Jesus. Hence Isaiah proclaims

48

'Here is your God; He comes with power; He comes like a shepherd feeding his flock' (Is 40:10). It happened in the ocean: a little fish said to an older one, 'Excuse me, you are older than I, so can you tell me where to find the thing they call the ocean?' 'The ocean is the thing you are in now,' replied the older one. 'Oh, this? But this is water. What I am seeking is the ocean,' said the disappointed fish, as he swam away to search elsewhere. How many of us are looking elsewhere for better life, when we are actually living in the ocean of God's presence, which is bliss itself!

In order to experience God who is with us, we need to go for a 'Desert Experience' like St John the Baptist, who was a voice in the desert heralding the Lord's coming (Mk 1:4). I do not mean that we must go into a physical desert, but to any place where we can be alone with God and pray: a corner in the backyard, a nook in the basement or a park bench. To pray one requires certain aids. First is simplicity. In city life we are easily enchanted by what is pretty, plastic and superficial. In order to pray, we have to get rid of this excessive baggage, because it blocks our way to Christ and to see things as they are. The second aid is silence. We need to be still, to be healed of our disturbed spirits. We need a place of quiet in order to calm our tingling nerves and hear God speak. The third is solitude. We cannot allow ourselves to be driven all the time by an instinct to perform, to produce and to do many things. Sometimes we have to stand alone in solitude to discover who we are and who our God is.

Going for a desert experience in order to experience God, like John, also means that like him we take a Camel Hair Route. John was clothed in camel hair, wore a leather belt and ate grasshoppers, thus appearing strange to his contemporaries. He was not trying to attract their attention; rather he was departing from the ordinary norms of society in order to jolt himself from the dullness of conformity. He was deliberately choosing a different experience to see if such an experience gave the intoxicating experience of God. It did. Likewise, we too must sometimes experience what it is like to be outside the ordinary pattern of human behaviour. For example, what would it feel like not 'to keep up with the Joneses' in the suburbs? What would it feel like to eat a few meagre meals one week in order to understand world hunger? What would it feel like to give one tenth of all that one owns to charity? What would it feel like to ration the use of one's car, in order to comprehend the energy crisis?

This Advent we need a symbolic desert experience in order to be aware of God, who is already here. 'Here I am with you', says God, 'and you keep thinking of me, talking of me with your tongue and searching for me in books! When will you shut up and see?' St Thomas Aquinas, one of the world's ablest theologians, suddenly stopped writing. When his secretary complained about his unfinished work, Thomas replied: 'Brother Reginald, some time ago I experienced something of the Absolute, so all I have written of God seems to me now like straw'. How could it be otherwise?

Let us pray.

Late I have loved Thee, O Beauty so ancient and so new; behold Thou were within me, and I outside, and I sought Thee outside; and in my unloveliness fell upon those lovely things that Thou hast made. Thou were with me and I was not with Thee, I was kept from Thee by those things; yet had they not been in Thee, they would not have been at all.

Thou didst call and cry to me to break open my deafness: and Thou didst send forth Thy beams and shine upon me and chase away my blindness: Thou did breathe fragrance upon me, and I drew in my breath and do now pant for Thee. I tasted Thee, and now hunger and thirst for Thee.

Thou did touch me, and I have burned for Thy peace.

St Augustine, 354-450

3rd Sunday of Advent, B

THERE IS ONE AMONG YOU

Isaiah 61:1-2, 10-11; 1 Thess 5:16-24; John 1:6-8,19-28

Theme : We are called to straighten up the rough and rugged spots in our lives so that, Jesus who stands always in our midst, can have easy entrance into our hearts with his joy and peace.

WE HEAR PEOPLE SAYING TO US 'WE MUST PUT GOD IN OUR LIVES'. But God is already here! Our business is to recognise Him. The gold necklace we wish to acquire is around our neck. 'There is one among you, whom you do not recognise' (Jn 1:26), said John the Baptist, pointing to the physical presence of Christ. The same Lord is now present in our midst in a mysterious way. It is his continued presence, though invisible, that gladdens our hearts, even amidst our shade and sadness. The sweet mark of a Christian is not faith, not even love, but joy, because we are all strings in the concert of His joy. Did not the angel announce at the birth of Jesus, 'I bring you glad tidings of great joy?' So St Paul asks us to 'rejoice always' (1 Thess 5:16) and Isaiah shouts out, 'I rejoice heartily in the Lord, the joy of my soul' (Is 61:10). Joy is never within our power as pleasure is. Only Christ can fill us with joy. Joy is the flag which is flown from the castle of the heart when the King is in residence there.

Jesus, ever present, enters our hearts in the silence of prayer, provided we do not resist him by hiding behind layers of distractions, drowning his voice with noise from television sets and stereos. He comes to us through his words in the scriptures. If we listen to his words in Sunday readings, not like listening to a cassette rerun, his words will come alive, questioning and enlightening our minds, challenging and testing our wills, moving and inspiring our hearts. He comes through the sacraments, which are those intense moments of grace and peak experiences of God. There are many other ways in which the Lord comes into our lives. He is always behind the scenes, but He moves all the scenes He is behind.

But we need to 'make straight the way of the Lord' (Jn 1:23). Not that we must strew roses, roses all the way, but at least we must not throw thorns and thistles and block his way. One sure block that obstructs his way is pride. Pride is a 'psychological inflation', more disastrous than what economic experts call 'run-away inflation'; the latter only deprives people of adequate purchasing power, but the former deprives Jesus of any space in a human heart that is swollen from an exaggerated idea of self-importance. Although Jesus himself said that 'John the Baptiser was greater than any man born of a woman, John was so humble that he felt unworthy 'even to untie his sandal strap' (Jn 1:27). Pride and grace dwelt never in one place.

A set lifestyle one may cling to, against the constant warning of Christian consicence, could also hinder the coming of Christ into our hearts. A crow once flew in the sky with a piece of meat in its beak. Twenty other crows set out in hot pursuit and began to attack it viciously. When the crow finally dropped the meat the pursuers left it alone and flew off shrieking after the morsel. Said the crow, 'I have lost the meat but gained this peaceful sky'. Likewise, when we drop from our lives 'that something' which is un-Christian, the peace of Christ flows into our hearts. Of course, the most common stumbling block that impedes the coming of Christ is selfishness. It is only when my selfish house is burnt down that I get an unobstructed view of the moon at night. Advent calls us to straighten up those rough and rugged spots in our lives, so that Jesus can have an easy entrance; to work quietly on the chunks of darkness hidden within us, in order to make way to the light of Christ; and to get in tune with all the mysterious ways Christ comes, so that, when he comes we can recognise him. We obtain salvation, not through action, nor through meditation, but through recognition.

Let us pray,
Father in heaven,
the day draws near when the glory of your Son
will make radiant the night of the waiting world.
May the lure of greed not impede us from the joy
which moves the hearts of those who seek him.
May the darkness not blind us
to the visions of wisdom
which fills the minds of those who find him.

Roman Missal: Opening Prayer for the 2nd Sunday of Advent

4th Sunday of Advent, B

HIGHLY FAVOURED DAUGHTER

2 Sam 7:1-5, 8 -11 Rom 16:25-27: Lk :26-38

Theme : Like Mary, if we believe and obey God's word, we too can conceive Christ spiritually and make him present in the world.

HUMANKIND'S GREATEST WISDOM IS TO KNOW THAT GOD SENT His Son into this world to break the chains of sin; humankind's greatest joy is to possess the peace of Christ, which makes 'the heart to swell with rapture'; humankind's greatest blessing is to hope that beyond the grave the followers of Jesus shall reign above the sun. God bestowed on Mary every favour that is the greatest in the order of grace. Whether the sun was shining or the sky was black, Mary was always led by His grace. A little fish in the Thames once became suddenly apprehensive lest by drinking so many pints of water in the river each day, it might drink the Thames dry. But father Thames said to it: 'Drink away, little fish, my stream is sufficient for thee'. Likewise, Father in heaven kept constantly assuring Mary 'My grace is sufficient for thee'. Why the extraordinary favour done to Mary alone? Because, as St Paul tells the Romans, 'when the mystery of Jesus Christ, hidden for many ages, was finally revealed, God expected mankind to believe and obey' (Rom 16:25), and Mary was the first disciple of Christ to believe and obey.

Mary believed. Her faith was humble and hence she first believed and only then reasoned upon it. 'What a piece of work is man! How noble is his reason.' Yes, God wanted Mary to submit even that noble reason to faith. A man was dangerously hanging on to a single branch on the top of a tree from where he could not climb down. He cried out to God, 'Oh, God, save me; you know I believe in you. All that I ask of you is to save me and I shall proclaim your name to the ends Of the earth'. 'Very well', said the voice Of God, 'I shall save you. Let go of that branch'. The distraught man yelled out, 'Let go of this branch? Do you think I am crazy?' Some people cling to their reason so ada-mantly that they are never able to see the light of faith. Mary's faith was ever active, so she not only accepted the divine truth but dwelt upon it, used it and developed it. Her faith was ever active and hence 'the handmaid of the Lord' did not exclude even death from her faith. Whatever is alive must die. Look at the flowers; only plastic flowers never die.

Mary obeyed. Her obedience was risk-taking. When she said, 'Let it be done according to thy word' (Lk 1:38), She did not realise the full implication of the 'word'. Words are inad-equate reflections of reality. How can a man claim to know what Niagara Falls are like, just because he has seen Niagara water in a bucket? Her obedience was loving. She loved God and so she trusted in Him and obeyed. After all, the important religious distinction is not between those who worship and those who do not worship, but between those who love and those who don't. Mary's obedience was persevering. God the supreme Artist, who painted a picture of stunning beauty on her, not only brought her joy, meaning and hope through splashes of colour; but also smeared on her lily white soul, black and ugly stains of pain and hardships. And yet, Mary kept on saying 'yes' to Him, till the end of her earthly story.

The Messiah as foretold by prophet Nathan to King David in the book of Samuel, had already come in the person of Jesus, fulfilling the messianic hopes of all nations. Now, He wants to come into each one of us individually at Christmas. However sinful we may be, He still invites us to His birthday party, for 'nothing is impossible for God' (Lk 7 :37). But at the party He will challenge us, as He challenged Mary, to accept the role God has designed for each of us in life. Like Mary, if we believe and obey His word, we can also make Christ present within us, and through us His light can illumine the world.

Let us pray,
Blessed Virgin, God's highly favoured daughter, you were heaven when you held heaven's Prince in your womb;
It is that heaven now to which we aspire, that flames may unite with flames.
The gates of paradise were closed to humankind because of Eve, but they opened again because of you; You are blessed!
Corruption could not blemish you and death could not contain you.
God clothed you in the garments of salvation, like a bride adorned in her jewels.
Eternal word found a dwelling place in your living flesh,
God made you the sanctuary of his presence and the temple of his Spirit,
Fill the hearts of your children with the hope of Christ's glory.
Make us too, bearers of his Spirit in mind, heart and body.
May we be saved by the mystery of Christ's redemption and share in your glory.

Christmas Day - a second look

STANDING BEFORE THE CRIB

Isaiah 52:7-10; Hebrews 1: 1-6; John 1:1-18

Theme: Standing before the crib we see Jesus, observe and hear Mary and Joseph what they are doing and saying, and receive the divine light they shed on our lives as we bow in humble worship.

I see child Jesus. In him I see God who has lavished His generosity towards me. But when I look at myself, I am ashamed to see a kindergarten heart in an adult body. In him, I see a God who humbled himself to my human level. But I have been like an empty vessel which rattles its small coins noisily. I see Mary. She is beautiful, on the goodness of her heart. Beauty without goodness is worse than wine and will intoxicate the holder and the beholder. I see Joseph. He is silent even when Mary is near. This silence is not the absence of sound but of self. Both have surrendered themselves to God in the manger. Our world regards silence as a deficiency, so some radios, even on Christmas Eve, keep us awake until dawn, playing ' Silent Night'.

I observe around the crib. I don't see any sign of modern civilisation. There is not even a door or a window, which we moderns keep shut, even during the day time.

There is no watchdog of the kind that welcomes guests entering a modern house by barking, if not biting them. Mary is not wearing slacks, which is not slack enough these days. Joseph is not smoking a cigarette, while some ultra-moderns consume three packets a day, as if they contained all the Vitamins. And yet, though civilized things are absent from the crib, we have here the first civilized persons in the world: Jesus, Mary, Joseph. After all, what use are civilized things without civilized individuals? Twenty-five civilisations before ours, have been destroyed, not by enemies from outside, but by people inside.

I hear Mary telling Joseph, 'I hear people gossip about us, having a baby without living together as husband and wife'. Joseph says 'Don't worry, Mary. Worry never accomplishes anything, except wrinkles, which gives another thing to worry about. Leave gossip alone; those who gossip are caught in their own mouth-trap'.

Mary says, 'God could have given us at least a cradle for the baby'. Joseph says, 'My dear, at least we have this crib. Some people are so poor that even cockroaches shun them. One advantage of being poor is that it does not cost much. And those who sleep on the floor never fall out of bed; riches are not always blessings'. Mary says, 'Joseph, don't speak loudly; the baby is sleeping'. Joseph says, 'Yes, we mustn't disturb him. He sleeps so soundly even in poor swaddling clothes'. Of course, man's conscience and not his mattress has most to do with his sleep.

I touch the floor of the crib. It is very cold. We people have become so cold towards one another that God has become man to warm us up. Often, we are neither cold nor hot, but lukewarm, and a lukewarm Christian makes a good bench-warmer although a poor heart-warmer. I kiss the feet of the child Jesus. All the legislation in the world cannot abolish kissing. The word 'kiss' was invented by poets to rhyme with bliss. So when I kiss Jesus I kiss the eternal bliss. but I must take care that I do not kiss as Judas did.

Let us pray.
It is very meet and right and just for salvation,
that we should at all times and in all places
give thanks unto Thee; O Lord, Holy Father;
because through the mystery of the Incarnate Lord,
the light of Thy glory hath shone anew upon the eyes of our minds:
that while we acknowledge God made visible,
we may be caught up through him to the love of things invisible
and therefore with angels and archangels,
with thrones and dominations and with the hosts of the heavenly army
we sing the hymn of thy glory.

Preface of the Nativity, Roman Missal

1st Sunday of Lent, B

LENT IS LOVABLE

Genesis 9:8-15, 3:1-7; I Pet 3:18-22; Mark 1:12-15

Theme : Lent is meant to be enjoyed, not to be endured, for it invites us to begin again, to grow into maturity and to emerge spiritually stronger through self-discipline.

O NE COULD LOVE LENT. LIKE ALL LOVABLE THINGS, Lent is meant to be enjoyed rather than to be endured. No matter what kind of a mess we have made of things up to this point, Lent once again offers us an opportunity to leave our past behind and start again. We may have broken our last lenten resolutions; but a lovers' quarrel is the renewal of love. So, Lent invites us to begin again and renew. This is the wonderful thing about Christian life: it is a series of new beginnings. We can always start again. Like the gardeners who every year plant new seeds to see blooms in May, we are invited to sow seeds of God's words deep within our hearts during Lent, to reap Easter fruits in abundance.

Lent is a growing period. We grow by giving a mature response to God's covenantal love which rings aloud in His promise, dressed in in symbolic language, 'I set my bow in the clouds to serve as the sign of the eternal covenant between me and the earth. never again shall a flood shall destroy all mortal beings' (Gen 9:12-13). God fulfilled His promise when Jesus died on the cross and rose again. 'This is why Christ died for sins once for all so that he could lead you to God' (1 Pet.3:18). This means that whatever our experience of the power of evil, that is not to be our final story. God intends life for us, not death. We grow during Lent by accepting this 'Good News'. No matter how much the power of sin and its effects have flooded every area of our lives, salvation is possible for those who enter the ark and separate themselves from evil.

Lent is a training period. It trains us to combat evil through desert experience, as Jesus himself did for forty days (Mk.1:12). There are desert areas in our lives where decisions are needed and resolutions must be made. Often the very thing which would release God's power in us is the very thing we avoid. Christ asks us to look into the wilderness of our innermost self, where there are no kindly friends to colour our faults with soothing words. Christ asks us to see ourselves as we really are, and rid ourselves of anything ungodly and unchristian, saying, 'This is the time of fulfilment. Reform your lives' (Lk.1:12). Lent, therefore, offers a period of self-discipline. Self-discipline never means *giving up* anything; in self discipline, we are not giving up the things of the earth, we are only exchanging them for better things. Discipline hurts. Yes. There will always be some initial pain in reforming our lives. Even children, learning to play the guitar, feel initial pain by pressing their fingers against the strings! Thus, trained by Lent, we would emerge spiritually strong, as Jesus emerged from the desert, as a wiry athlete ready for the ultimate test of his strength in the struggle against evil. Our Lord's struggle against evil still goes on, but now the battle ground has shifted from the desert into our own spirits.

Let us begin Lent with confidence, because whether we gaze

with longing into the garden or with fear into the desert, God walked there first. Let us begin Lent with hope, because the symbols of ashes and purple and sombreness of Lent will soon be eclipsed by the light and flowers and alleluias of the Easter season, as the drab and darkness of winter will be transformed into the colour and promise of spring. Let us begin Lent with enthusiasm, because although the things we do for Lent - our fasting, abstinence, prayer and works of charity - may indeed be small, they are important victories for the kingdom of God and defeats for the evil present in our lives. Hence, we must make love, not war, with Lent; and in love, there is always one who kisses and one who offers the cheek. Lent offers its cheek, but are we prepared to kiss ?

Let us pray
O Lord our God, you formed us from the clay of earth
and breathed into us the spirit of life,
yet, we have turned from your face and sinned.
But we are now ready to repair and compose in the little ship of our soul,
whatever has been broken or ruined by the stormy waves of sins.
Save us, O God, for the waters have come up to our neck,
and we are sinking in deep mire where there is no foothold.
Grant to us to begin our christian warfare with holy fasts and prayer,
Laying aside all memories of evil, we cry to you.
May we wash ourselves with tears, for your divine purification.
May we pray to behold the fulfilment of your revelation.
May we prepare for adoring the cross and the resurrection of Jesus.

2nd Sunday of Lent, B

HE TOUCHED ME

Genesis 22 :1-2, 9-18; Rom 8:31-34; Mark 9:2-10

Theme: If we take ourselves to prayer as often as we can, we too, like Christ can have our own moments of transfigurations, when the touch of God could lift our darkness and melt away our fears.

SCIENCE COMMITS SUICIDE IF IT DENIES GOD. It cannot deny, for the supernatural is not its field of enquiry. However, many moderns, influenced by science, dismiss the reality of the Spirit as primitive myth. But Jesus by his Transfiguration revealed that God is indeed real; because what happened at the Transfiguration of Christ was only the explosion of the Spirit already present in him, breaking through with brilliance, giving him a rare glimpse of God's face, transporting him for a while to the realm of pure spirits and touching the chords of the ineffable joy within him.

Such a transfiguration, but in an imperfect manner, could happen to any human being, because God is an unutterable sigh planted in the depth of every human heart. It could happen to any Christian because God indwells by His Spirit in every soul redeemed by Christ. It actually happens to saints. Touched by God, St Paul challenged, 'When God is with us, who can be against us?' (Rom. 8.3). Touched by God, St Augustine exclaimed, ' Our hearts are made for you, Oh, God, and they shall not rest until they rest in you'. Touched by God, St Francis of Assisi sang, ' Make me a channel of your peace'. So, God can touch any heart that opens its doors to His love. Even an alcoholic when moved by the concern of a beloved wife, or a lonely and bereaved widow when comforted by the concern of a caring relative, or a confused and depressed young man when received by a kindly elder, could experience their moments of limited transfiguration; for it is the same transforming power of God which is transmitted when someone tells another 'I love you'.

At such moments of our own imperfect transfiguration, wonderful things can happen to us. For example, our attitude to suffering could change, for then we will realise that here on earth we can't walk in a straight line to victory and that the destiny of every Christian is written between two mountains, Calvary and Mount Tabor. Even Jane Torvill would testify that Olympic medals for ice dancing are not won simply by eating wheaties. We will also realise that even calamities can bring us blessings in the end; as to a bird who shelters each day in the branches of a withered tree which is suddenly uprooted by a whirlwind, forcing the bird to fly a hundred miles until it finally comes to a forest of fruit-laden trees. The touch of God could lift our darkness and melt away our fears, for all fear is bondage. We fear even love and that is why, we fear sacrifices, which was not the case for Abraham to whom even sacrificing his only son was meaningful because he loved God (Gen.22:9-10). Without meaning, sacrifices can destroy us, but if they do have meaning they can transform us.

But one thing is certain. If we want to have our transfigura-tions, we must have our Tabors, namely we must take ourselves to prayer. It was when Jesus climbed the Mount to pray that he was transfigured and heard 'You are my beloved son, in whom I am well pleased' (Mk.9:7). At prayer, the Lord will speak and we must 'listen to him' (Mk 9:7). The Lord may speak to us in any manner, either by putting an idea in our mind, or giving us a new perspective of life; by stirring up new desires in our heart, or by calming our turbulent emotions, or by actually whispering words to the listening ears of our souls. But in whatever manner he speaks, if only we listen, we will be transfigured, reborn and healed. Such a healing as comes from the touch of God can never be promised by the most reputable therapist of clinical psycho-therapy. The healing touch of God will kindle in our heart such a spark of hope and love, that we can go forward into our dark future, carrying an invisible lamp burning in our heart, pro-claiming to the rest of the world, ' He touched me'.

Let us pray.
Dear Lord Jesus, when you were transfigured, your disciples beheld your glory,
  so that they should not be afraid to see you on Calvary,
  for it would be only a prelude to your Easter glory.
As christans, our destiny too is written between two rnountains,
  frorn calvary to the mountain of transfiguration.
.May we forsake the indulgence of our flesh and take our share of suffering
  that the gifts of your Spirit may aid us to ascent to the mountain of Easter.
Your continued presence with us can take charge of every thing in us,
  transfiguring even that which disturbs us,
  penetrating even the hardened and incredulous regions within us,
  Take away the veil of our heart and free us from the darkness
  that shadows our vision, so that we see your face and hear your word.

3rd Sunday of Lent, B

BACK TO BASICS

Exodus 20:1-17 ; I Cor 1:22-25; John 2: 13-35

Theme: A loving and obedient relationship with God, an enduring reliance on Him for one's own fulfilment and a progressive renewal of heart are basics to Christian life.

ROOTS ARE BASICS TO TREES. Foundations are basic to buildings. Principles are basic to religion! It is easier to fight for basics than to live up to them; but that does not mean that we can give them up. A religion takes its eternal motivation from its basic principles. Hence 'Back to Basics' can serve us as a relevant Lenten campaign. This Sunday's Scriptural readings call us back to three important basic principles of Christian life.

First comes relationship. Christianity is not just a religion, it is a relationship. The essence of the ethics of Jesus is not law but a relationship of person to God. God gave us Ten Commandments (Ex.20:1-17), and we are told that, since the beginning of civilization, millions and millions of laws have not improved on them one bit. However, we would be fooling ourselves if we hope that the evils of this world can be cured by commandments or legislation. Only goodness within ourselves can achieve that. But for a human being to be good, he must be in relationship with God, for 'God alone is good'. Commandments were given to us, not to enslave us but to free us for love-relationship with

God. A Catholic who comes to Mass simply because he is obliged to is still a slave of the law. A Catholic who never comes to Mass because he thinks that the Spirit has freed him from all external laws, needs to ask himself what he really wants, God's will or his own. A Catholic who loves God would come to mass anyway, law or no law. Let us strike a loving relationship with God, who dwells in the deep well within us. It is sad that in some cases sins, like stones and grit, block that well; so much, that God is buried beneath and He has to be dug out.

Second comes Reliance. Reliance on God is more basic to our fulfilment than dependence on material things. No doubt, money is the sixth sense which enables us to enjoy the other five. But the picture of the merchants being driven out by Jesus from the Temple (Jn.2:13-25), warns us of preoccupation with money. Cattle, sheep, hay and corn can be bought in the 'Market Place'; but only in the 'Father's House' can we find deep peace. Reliance on one's own way of looking at things could also endanger our salvation, as was the case with Greeks and Jews, about whom St Paul writes. The Greeks expected Jesus to be another Plato, offering a new package of ideas in answer to the problems of evil and death. But Jesus did not. The Jews thought that for God to become man and be crucified on the cross was madness. And yet in the end 'God's folly was wiser than men and His weakness more powerful than men' (1 Cor 1 :23). How can we forget that we, who were deceived by the wisdom of the serpent, were 'freed by the foolishness of God?'

Third comes Renewal. Religion is in the heart, not in the knees. Hence progress in faith-journey supposes a progressive change of heart, which alone is true renewal. A person who can't change his own heart cannot change anything. If I cannot protect my own feet with slippers, how can I carpet the whole earth? A change of heart brings about purification of motives. If the world understood our motives, we should all, at times, be ashamed of our finest actions. Thank goodness the world cannot see. But the Lord can: 'Jesus was well aware of what was in a man's heart' (Jn.2:25). Jesus drove out the people who were doing business in the Temple, not simply because it was business - for even as business, it was a valuable service at a Feast - but because their motive was diluted by their manipulative intention, to make a 'fast buck'. Hence during Lent, let us aim at the renewal of our hearts. With God's help, all of us can. For the almighty God who drew out a fountain of water in the desert for His people, can draw from our hearts, however hard, tears of compunction.

Let us pray
God our Father, we have received Lent with gladness,
for with it the beginning of spiritual warfare arrived.
During this holy season, we want to fight our way
back to the basics, the foundation of christian life.
We want to deepen our loving relationship with each other;
Help us to lay bear to you our consciences that have grown bitter and hateful
and obtain your mercy that delights to spare;
We want to strengthen our dependence on you:
Hence, during this lenten season of deeper thought and graver song,
help us our ailing souls to grow well and strong.
We want to arouse ourselves to conversion of our inner most being.
During this feast of penance, may our spirits shine bright
with true conversion's heavenly light, like sunrise after stormy night.

4th Sunday of Lent, B

THE CHAOS OF THE CROSS

2 Chronicles 36:14-23; Eph 2:4-10; John 3:14-21

Theme: At the chaotic moments of our life, if we pray and reflect under the shadow of the cross of Christ, our dark days will become great days, for the Providence of God presides over human affairs.

THERE IS A DIVINITY THAT SHAPES OUR DESTINY. Men may cast their lots, gamble with their deeds, create chaos and confusion in the world and move the wheels of history with blood-stained hands. But the providence of God that presides over human lives finally brings about order out of chaos. The history of Israel was largely a history of chaos. The Jews suffered the collapse at the hands of a foreign power, were deported to exile and 'By the streams of Babylon they sat and wept' (Ps 137). However, just when it seemed as if all were over for them, King Cyrus of Persia, inspired by God, not only released them from exile but helped them rebuild their Temple (2 Chron. 36:20-23). Thus, God's mercy overcame His own wrath, drawing His people through their chaotic history closer to Himself.

The chaotic history of Israel repeated itself in the life of Jesus. Every time history repeats itself, the price goes up. The chaos of the cross became the ultimate chaos in human history, because on it, goodness itself was crucified as a common criminal. But once again God drew life out of that bleeding cross, so that it was

by the cross we were all saved, 'when we were dead in sin'
(Eph.2:4); and what a glorious and universal salvation that was!
The Son of Man was lifted upon the cross, so that everyone who
believes may have eternal life in him' (Jn.3:14). It is the same
cross which, until today, stands tall and high, in the hearts of
millions who continue to sing, 'nearer my God to Thee, nearer
to Thee! Even though it be a cross that raiseth me'.

This means that the history of the chaos of the cross is not
contained in thick books but lives in our very blood. We have
our own chaotic moments in life, but through them all 'God
intends to bring us to life and to make us truly his handiwork,
created to lead the life of good deeds' (Eph.2:8-10). We have
heard it said, 'Where there is life there is hope'. But we
Christians who believe in the power of the cross dare say 'Where
there is death there is life'. It is because we believe that the
crucified Christ lives with us that we hope, that in times of crisis
God will help us find a way to survive; that when we face
difficulties, He will help us devise ways to overcome them; that
when tragedies like fire or flood devastate our homes, He will
help to rebuild; that when our precious dreams are destroyed by
a mistake, He will inspire us to start over again; that there is
always hope even for a family where all love between the
members seems to have died and that there is always the hope
for a better future, for people who suffer under severe economic
and social conditions. Yes: order will always emerge from chaos;
new life will always spring from the Cross. This is our faith.

But this faith is a gift from God, not given to us on a plate,
but planted within us like a seed which must grow. It will grow
not when we grow more successful and wealthier in life, but
when we stand at the foot of the Cross and prayerfully reflect
upon the chaos of our life. For it is during such prayer and

reflection, our faith will deepen, to the extent that even death will appear, not as a going down but as a going up; not a crumbling into dust but a skyward sweep. As a result, our weeping may endure for a night but joy will come in the morning; life will no more be like 'a tale told by an idiot full of sound and fury, signifying nothing', as it did to Macbeth. We may be in the midst of winter but at prayer we will learn that there is in us an invincible summer. As long as we pray and reflect, on the confusion and convulsions of our life, under the shadow of the Cross, our dark days will become great days. Hence, of this let us be certain: the well of Providence is deep and the buckets we bring to it must not be small.

> Let us pray.
> When I survey the wondrous cross
>   on which the Prince of Glory died,
>   my richest gain I count but loss
>   and pour contempt on all my pride.
>
> Forbid it, Lord, that I should boast
>   save in the death of Christ my God;
>   all the vain things that charm me most,
>   I sacrifice them to his blood
>
> See from his head, his hands, his feet,
>   sorrow and love flow mingled down;
>   did e'er such love and sorrow meet
>   or thorns compose so rich a crown?
>
> Were the whole realm of nature mine,
>   that were an offering too small;
>   love so amazing, so divine,
>   demands my soul, my life, my all.

Isaac Watts

5th Sunday of Lent, B

BE NOT AFRAID

Jeremiah 31:31-34; Hebrews 5:7-9; John 12:20-33

Theme: Fearless dying to one's will and self-seeking, in obedience to God's will, preserves one's life for eternity; for life is fruitful in the measure in which it is laid out.

ONCE A SCHOOLBOY WAS ASKED WHAT PARTS OF SPEECH MY and MINE were. He answered that they were aggressive pronouns. How true he was! As a heavily laden cart goes creaking, so our 'self' mounted by its 'ego' often goes groaning. Alas, we are all serving a life sentence in the dungeon of self. Jesus came to show the way out of this dungeon; but the way he showed is puzzling. He said , 'The one who loves his life loses it, while the one who hates his life in this world preserves it to life eternal' (Jn.12:25). It is a paradox and a bitter one; Jesus lost many of his followers because of such bitter sayings. He was a poor P.R. man, but then he came not to please but to lead. Only politicians stand for what they think the voters will fall for; but Jesus was not a politician and hence He spoke only the Truth.

Jesus taught us to yield up the love of life for the sake of the life of love. What he taught, he also practised. He suffered the shame and pain of the cross, to die for the life of his foes. Because he died, his life lives on in untold souls. In a way, we are in debt to Adam, the first benefactor of our race, for bringing death into the world. Because Jesus died, his seed prevails, filling the earth, as

72

the stars fill the sky; his pain is our peace and his death is our life.

The paradox of life through death would not puzzle us so much, if we look at the nature and human growth. A seed lies smothered and submerged in the dark earth before it blooms and blossoms. The whole future of that seed remains unfulfilled, if it is not buried in earth to die (Jn.12:24). Look at any sphere of human life. By putting to death the traditional forms of expression in art, music and literature some artists gave birth to new forms; by putting to an end to transportation by horse and buggy, conveyance by automobile came in; by putting to rest the Old Testament ritual of circumcision, Jews became Christians; by burying the Latin liturgy of the Middle ages, vernacular mass was born; by their deaths, Mahatma Gandhi in India and Martin Luther King in America became powerful influences in the liberation of their people; by dying to some of our old attitudes and forms of behaviour we embark on a new way of life.

Therefore, as Jesus told us, life is fruitful in the measure in which it is laid down. Our highest life does not consist in self-expression but in self-sacrifice. It is not what we take up but what we give up that makes us and others rich. Do we want eternal Spring in our heart? Then we must welcome winter on our head. Do we want to enjoy the glory of sunshine? Then we must live through the night and death. If we are afraid of death, probably we are afraid of life as well.

Dying to self would often mean sacrificing our self-will, for the sake of God's will, which is His Law ' placed within us and written upon our hearts' (Jer 31:33). God wills only our good, hence the greatest of His Laws is our greatest good. Nine-tenths of our difficulties are overcome when our heart obeys God's will. The mother and guardian of all virtues is obedience. That is why, summing up Jesus's thirty years of hidden life, the gospel says, 'He was subject to them' and that to the end 'Son though he was, he learned obedience from what he suffered' (Heb 5:8).

We give God very little when we give Him our possessions; but when we give Him our own will, we give Him ourselves; and in any giving, only when we give of ourselves do we truly live. Besides, if we deliberately sacrifice our own will for that of God, He, with all His mighty power, will ordain the remotest star, and the last grain of sand, to assist us.

Of course, dying to self very often means sacrificing ourselves for the sake of others. Only by dying to our self-seeking and vain ambitions can we bring life to others, spreading joy and inspiring hope. Like Jesus, many heroic men and women found love for God and neighbour as values worth dying for. If one has found nothing worth dying for, then he or she has probably found nothing worth living for. Let us not be afraid of such dying before we actually die. For death is only a parting of the cloud, which hides the sun.

Let us pray.
Lord Jesus, you ask us to lose our life for your sake,
which leaves us staggered and bewildered by its sheer incredibility,
for, of all the possessions we have, the most valuable is life.
But we understand.
You want us to die to sin so that we may rise to eternal life.
to be ready to suffer for faith, so that we may inherit the kingdom.
to carry our daily crosses in life, so that we can grow wise and mature,
to work in the service of the poor, so that we may prove our love for God.
Although dying to oneself will be really hard, we are not afraid.
Your grace won by your death on the cross is always available to help us.
Your grace is omnipotence that acts redemptively, Give us your grace.
Your grace is a sure beginning of glory in us; Give us your grace.
We can do nothing right without your grace, Give us your grace.

Passion Sunday, B

AT THE FOOT OF THE CROSS

Isaiah 50:4-7; Philippians 2:6 -11; Mark 14:1-15:47

Theme: Standing at the foot of the cross, we marvel at the incomparable Christ, thank him for his indefatigable love, feel sorry for paining him with our sins, and pray for selfless love.

LORD, I MARVEL AT YOU. YOU ARE INCOMPARABLE. In infancy you startled a king; in boyhood you puzzled the learned doctors; in manhood you walked upon the waves and hushed the sea to sleep; and finally you hung upon the cross and broke the sting of death. Great men have come and gone, but you live on. Herod could not kill you, Satan could not seduce you, death could not destroy you and the grave could not hold you. You are incredible. You never wrote a book but more books have been written on you than on anyone else. You never wrote a song but you provided a theme for the best musicians in the world. You never practised medicine but you have healed more broken hearts than any other physician. All this by your death on the cross. Like the flower that blooms and in blooming it dies, like the pelican that was thought to feed its young ones with its blood and, in feeding, die, you died giving life.

Lord, I THANK YOU. I thank you for the poverty, the pains and the passion you suffered for me. You slept in a borrowed manger, you cruised on the lake in a borrowed boat and were buried in a borrowed tomb. You are the maker of the universe and yet you were made a curse on the cross. Your holy fingers made the meadows yet they grew the thorns that crowned your head. You made the forests yet they gave the tree upon which you hung. You made the sky, but it darkened over your head when you died. It was for love of me you suffered all these. I can see upon the cross inscribed in shining letters: 'God is Love'. Yes, your love is so great, so vast, and so mighty that I may count the leaves of the forest trees or the sparkling drops of dew at the sunrise, but never can I tell the depth of your love. That is why it has lasted longest and stood the hardest test. I was born in my mother's pain and I will not perish in my own, because you love me.

Lord, I am SORRY. Evil men put you to death but that dark evil sleeps in me as well. Like the crowd that jubilantly sang 'Hosanna!' but soon turned into an angry mob shouting 'Crucify him!' I too have praised you with songs and pained you with sins. I have often twisted you with the fickleness of my human nature that cannot be consistent for two days in a row. It was Judas in me that betrayed my commitments to you; like Pilate who blew hot and cold in the same breath declaring you innocent but condemning you to death, I too have been a bundle of contradictions, believing one thing and practising another. Like Peter, I have been weak and cowardly. As he wept I want to weep: indeed, there are many tears in my heart but they never reach my eyes. Like the soldiers who crucified you on the excuse that they were simply carrying out orders, I too have been good at blaming others for my faults, and in doing so I have only made them the worse. Lord give me true repentance. I cannot repent too soon because I do not know how soon it would be too late. I know I am a sinner, but do not know how great; you alone know, for you died for my sins.

Lord, I PRAY. You have often pierced my mind with the arrows of your words; now pierce my heart with the arrows of your love. Let my love for you be selflessness: whenever I loved you right, I was virtuous; but whenever I loved you wrong, I sinned. Mend me, a bruised reed, so that this poor reed is tuned for you. Enter into my life more deeply; my life will be filled with meaning only when you enter into it. Hold me fast as I journey in faith; as I dare not let go of the rope while I climb a mountain, so I cannot let go of your hand as I climb the everlasting hills. You did not come to explain away suffering or remove it, but to fill it with your presence, so that the streams of my life become snow-white when they clash against the rocks. Be with me, therefore, when I suffer. I have heard you whispering in my pleasures but even when you shout in my pains, I have failed to hear you. Sharpen the ears of my heart to hear you saying, 'I am with you', and open the eyes of my soul, to see the Easter morning that lies just beyond Calvary.

Let us pray.

Lord Jesus Christ, you are the King of Israel, David's royal Son, who in God's name came as the blessed one.

As the people of the Hebrews went before you with palms we too present to you our praises, singing hosannas.

You accepted their praises and prayers: so too, we ask you to accept our praises and prayers.

Help us to follow your example by doing good to those who hurt us, by trusting in God while we suffer and by dying to our sins, so that, as you rose from the dead he too may rise to new life in you.

CYCLE C

1st Sunday of Advent, C

THE TIME IS NOW

Jer 33:14-16; 1 Thess 3: 12-4:2; Luke 21:25-28, 34-36

Theme: Advent is the time to start living a purposeful life, to watch and pray, to love and share, and to wait on the Lord with hope.

IT IS FASCINATING TO FIGURE OUT HOW THE END OF THE WORLD will come.

The Great Planet Earth, a book by Hal Lindsay, became a best-seller, selling over fifteen million copies, because it contained a set of staggering speculations about the end time. Jesus's own description of the end, with 'the roaring of the seas' and 'the heaven shaking' (Lk 21:25-26), might indeed be fascinating to some, but frightening to many. However, Jesus did not speak about the end of the world to scare us, although a good scare is, at times, worth more than good advice. Jesus who always said, 'Fear not' but 'believe', cannot speak of the end time to frighten us. He knew too well that fear imprisons, but faith liberates; fear paralyses, but faith empowers; and fear sickens, but faith heals. Hence Christ's purpose of describing the end was not to instil fear but to inspire us with the urgency of the gospel message.

The time for us to organise our lives with right priorities is NOW. On the night of 1st April 1912 the Titanic hit an iceberg in the North Atlantic and sank. Over fifteen hundred people lost their lives. Suppose I ask, 'If you had been on the Titanic when it sank, would you have rearranged the deckchairs?' Surely, you would say, that it is a ridiculous question; for who in his right mind, would ignore wailing sirens on a sinking ship and rearrange its deckchairs? But then, we know that our life on earth is so brief that in the midst of life, we are in death; that our world with all its display of pomp and glory is dissolving. And yet it is possible that some of us are so busy making a living, that we forget the purpose of living, 'allowing our spirits to become bloated with indulgence and worldly cares' (Lk 21.34). Is it not like rearranging deck chairs on a sinking ship?

The time is NOW, to 'watch and pray' (Lk 21 :36) so that prayer opens our eyes to the presence of God, helping us to see everything in proper perspective and implants in our hearts peace, even in the midst of problems and pains. Prayer is also listening to God's word. How eager we are to listen to the news. Our interest increases depending upon who reads it, for it adds a note of authority. Suppose I turn on TY and see God reading the news ! Surely, it would lift me out of my seat. And yet, it is God who speaks every word in the Scriptures. In the days to come, before Christmas, we will feel the powerful presence of God in his Word, provided we believe as Jeremiah did: ' See, the days are coming- it is the Lord who speak when I am going to fulfil the promise' (Jer 35:14)

The time is NOW, to love and share, in a true Christian way. When God became man, He brought all of us into a grand relationship not only with Himself but with our fellow men. There are no spinisters and bachelors in the kingdom of God. No Christian can walk alone, for he belongs. Hence if we want Christ to come into our lives in a living dynamic way, then during Advent our 'hearts must overflow with love for one another and for all' (1 Thes 3:12), lifting our spirit of sharing.

Sharing does not impoverish us, it only enriches us with a deep sense of satisfaction.

The time is NOW, to wait on the Lord and hope. Have you ever stood on a foreign airport, awaiting the arrival of a plane carrying someone you love; and after what seemed an interminable delay, how thrilled you were to see your loved one emerging, to complete your joy of reunion? Likewise, we await during Advent the coming of the Lord into our lives, with expectation, until our reunion with Him, hopefully becomes ecstacy at Christmas. During this waiting period we may experience the end of the world in our personal lives, when for example, a close relative dies or when marriage breaks down or when the job is gone or serious illness strikes; all of which can shake our world to its foundation. Even in these moments of desolation and distress, we are called ' to stand up straight and raise our hearts' (Lk 21:28), for the Lord is near.

> Let us pray,
> Father in heaven, may we realise that time is the most valuable thing we can spend in preparation for Christmas;
> Guard us against killing time, a killing which is not murder but is suicide.
> Give us grace to organise our lives and not to continue to live in darkness which is the mist of sin that hides your face.
> Watch over us who are still in our dangerous voyage exposed to the rough storms of troubles and temptations and steer the vessel of our life towards the everlasting shore of peace Grant that we may strive together, by loving and sharing extending to others what we so richly enjoy.
> Teach us to use all the circumstances of our life, so that they bring forth in us. the fruits of holiness and joy,
> rather than the fruits of sin and sadness.

2nd Sunday of Advent, C

THE JOY OF SALVATION

Baruch 5:1-9; Philippians 1:4-6, 11; Luke 3: 1-6

Theme: If we set right in our lives what needs to be set right, the Joy of Salvation will flood our hearts so much that we will be taking it to others.

IF THERE IS NO JOY IN BEING A CHRISTIAN, probably my Christianity is leaking some where. This joy has its springs deep down inside, and that spring is Christ. Yes, pleasure is in our power, joy is not. 'God, who is leading Israel in joy' does so 'by the light of his glory' (Bar 5:9), which is Jesus Christ. Anyone who comes in touch with Christ experiences this joy. Mother Teresa tells us of a young Maltese girl who joined her Order. On the first day she was sent to the Home for the Dying. When she came home she was radiant. Mother Teresa asked why she was so happy. The girl said, 'Mother, I have held Christ in my hands for three hours.'

It is for the coming of this Christ that we are waiting during Advent. Of course, Christ cannot come back in the way Mohammed Ali might stage a come-back, for Christ has been never away. He is always with us as he himself said. Hence, what we are waiting for is that Christ may reveal himself and make his presence felt in a new way giving us an intense experience of the joy of salvation.

However, the joy of salvation does not come to us by flashing a magic wand or pressing a Christmas button. Salvation is free, yes, but it is not cheap. We have to work for it, breaking the chains we have bound ourselves with. I don't mean the so-called deadly sins, the most expensive ones; but the disposition of our hearts that renders us incapable of even seeing this salvation, leave alone experiencing it. I mean the selfishness that stops us doing a kind act, the resentment that blocks the communication, the falsehood that betrays trust, the pride that precludes true regard for others, and the communal prejudice that can destroy a society. So John was right in repeating Isaiah's call to 'make ready the way of the Lord and clear him a straight path' (Lk 3:5). The least we could do at Advent is, not to put any spiritual obstacle for the Lord's coming. I once asked a born-again Christian friend how many it took to convert him. 'Two', he replied. 'Why two - did not God do it all?' I asked. 'The Almighty and myself converted me; I did all I could against it, and the Almighty did all He could, for it, and He won', he said.

The joy of salvation is not the private property of any Christian, in fact, the full value of joy is in sharing it with someone. Besides, it is not right for anyone to consume joy without producing it. Hence we are called to bring this joy to others also, first by promoting justice in the world. It was the dream of God our Father, that with the coming of His Son Jesus, His Church, the new Jerusalem, 'wrapped in the cloak of justice', would offer the world 'the peace of justice' (Bar 5:3); so that, 'all mankind shall see the salvation of God' (Lk 3:6). Hence it is the sacred duty of every Christian 'to promote the gospel', in such a way that the entire world 'may be found rich in the harvest of justice which Christ has ripened in us' (Phil 1:4-6). Are we, then, doing our part to level off the sharp peaks of greed and mountain-sized injustice in the world; and to fill in the low, cold areas of depression and despair, that millions suffer in the dark valleys of gap between the rich and the poor?

Now, I am afraid, you are beginning to wonder whether Advent is a joyful season or a penitential period; as the French proverb goes, 'Great joys weep and great sorrows laugh', for life itself is made up of marble and mud. It is true that Advent has joyous strains, but it also calls us to struggle in straightening up our lives, using the helps available. There is help through the sacraments, with an emphasis on reconciliation; there is help through prayer in which we sincerely seek the Lord; and there is help in Jesus's people around, through whom God speaks. The rough ways, the twisted roads and the steep paths are negotiable, for He is coming.

Let us pray,

Most Gracious God, whose will is joy for the afflicted, let your herald's urgent cry 'Prepare the Way of the Lord' pierce our hardened hearts, so that we ready ourselves for the dawn of your kingdom.

May our complacency give way to conversion, oppression to justice, and conflict to love of one another.

Help us fill the valley of our fears with courage, to live a new life in You;

Help us fill the valley of our weaknesses with strength, to break the bonds of sin;

Help us fill the valley of doubts with faith, to believe that, with your help, we cannot fail.

Give us the humility to level off the mountain of our mistaken dreams, conceited poses, and arrogant gestures of all the other pretences with which we hope to deceive ourselves and others.

Grant us the generosity we need for renunciation and surrender: the primary conditions for a fruitful and rewarding Advent.

3rd Sunday of Advent, C

CHEER UP

Zephaniah 3:14-18; Philippians 4:4-7; Luke 3.10-18

Theme : The Lord is coming to cheer us up and to renew in His love, provided We are prepared, to surrender our lives to Him.

IT HAS HAPPENED TO ME AT TIMES that when I have been in deep desolation, a friend has told me 'Cheer up, boy!' which has only made me go into deeper depression. But when God tells us, as He does now, two weeks before Christmas, 'Cheer up, shout for joy, be glad and exult', we actually tend to cheer up, for God's commands, unlike men's, are creative, bringing into effect what they say. Did He not say at the dawn of creation, 'Let there be light' and instantly the dark abyss of earth was flooded with light? In fact, God created us to be people always spilling over with joy, and hence He not only asks us to rejoice but wants Himself 'to sing joyfully because of us, as one sings at festivals' (Zeph 3:14-16). Can you imagine anything more crazy than this, that the Lord Himself is coming to lead us in our merry dance? So, we'd better all be on the floor to sing and rejoice, especially when we come for the solemn Sunday liturgies during Advent; let us come, not with long-faced solemnity, as though we lived behind Berlin Walls and Iron Curtains, which in any case have been pulled down.

We must rejoice because 'The Lord your God is already in

your midst' (Zeph 3:15). When the Lord became man He did not become just one man; in a sense, He became every man and every woman, dwelling closer to each of us than our thoughts and desires. Yes, we were born broken, but our life is mending, for God is acting in us like glue.

Besides, the Lord intends to come into our lives more intimately during this Christmas season, in order to 'renew us in His love' (Zeph 3.17). Is there any force more healing than that of love? Love always arrives with healing in its wings. It is the arrival of this Lord of love, in ever new ways, we now anticipate. The delight of children going to see Santa Claus, the buying and wrapping of Christmas gifts, the decorating of Christmas trees, all these Advent activities express this great anticipation of something wonderful about to happen.

The wonderful thing is, of course, is the 'Joy in the Lord'; a joy that comes not from any particular position in life but from the disposition of our hearts; a joy of the mind free of chains and heart free of blame; a joy born of conviction of faith and consciousness of God's love. Because this is a joy in the Lord, it is possible even to those who may find the Christmas season itself the most distressing because of the demands it makes and the tension it creates. Such a joy is possible even in the most trying of circumstances, even as we contemplate our present world which was once threatened by cold war but now by cold peace. This is why St Paul, although living in prison under the shadow of impending death, could encourage the early Christians, who themselves were under constant threat from political and military powers, saying, 'Rejoice in the Lord, I say it again rejoice' (Phil 4:4). This means, if my joy is in the Lord, I will smile even when I am chasing my best hat down the street on a windy day. Shall we then beg the Lord, that this Christmas may fill us with joy in him?

But whatsoever we beg of God, we must also work for it; our future will be different if we make our present different, but how? ' He who has two coats, let him share with him who has none, the man who has food should do the same' (Lk 3:11).. What does this mean? We are beautiful people, lovable people, but we are also vulnerable people, especially to selfishness. If in our selfishness, we are all the time receiving and not giving, we will be like the Dead Sea which is dead, because it is all the time getting, never giving out. To make way for the joy in the Lord also calls us to surrender ourselves to God in prayer. 'Have no anxiety about anything but if there is anything you need, pray' (Phil 4:6). To those who surrender to Him, somehow the good will be the final goal of their ills. Hence let us cheer up and charm it with a smile; one smile in public is worth ten before your mirrors, for it keeps joy in circulation.

> *Let us pray,*
> *O come, O come, Emmanuel,*
> *and ransom captive Israel,*
> *that mourns in lonely exile here*
> *until the Son of God appear*
> *Rejoice ! Rejoice ! Emmanuel shall come to Thee, O Israel.*
> *O come, thou Day Spring, come and cheer*
> *our spirits by thine Advent here;*
> *dispose the gloomy clouds of night*
> *and death's dark shadows put to flight.*
> *O come, O come, thou Lord of Might*
> *and open wide our heavenly home;*
> *make safe the way that leads on high.*
> *and close the path to misery.*
> *Rejoice. Rejoice. Emmanuel shall come to thee, Israel.*
> *O Antiphons (12th-13th century)*

4th Sunday of Advent

PEACE ON EARTH

Micah 5:1-4; Hebrews 10:5-10; Luke 1:39-45

Theme: Led by the Holy Spirit, if we live a life of loving union with God and neighbour, the Peace of Christ will flow like a river into our hearts, turning us into channels of Peace for the world.

EVER SINCE MASS BEGAN TO BE SAID IN OUR CHURCHES, we have been singing, 'Peace on Earth'. It is sad that after two thousand years of mass, we have got as far as poison gas. Even when a peace treaty is made, it often turns out to be a period of cheating between two periods of fighting. How can there be peace on earth, when there is no peace within individuals? Peace and joy are touches of sweet harmony within us, harmony between our body, mind and heart. When my instincts thunder out of my control, when reason runs wild and the heart desires only what is immoral, illegal and fattening, then I am like an atom whose electrons have broken free of the nucleus. This disunity within a person causes further disunity between man and man, with the result that one half of the human race is at war with the other half. But all these disunities are symptoms of the most tragic disunity which is the rupture between man and God; for God is like the hub of a wheel, and when the hub is lost the spokes of the wheel fall apart. Therefore, peace on earth will become a reality only when every human person is reunited with God.

It is in order to reunite all people with God and rest them at peace that Jesus came. At his birth angels sang, 'Peace to all of good-will'; but even before his birth the prophet foretold that 'He shall be Peace' (Mic 5:4). Hence wherever Jesus is, we can expect that sweet peace sits crowned with smiles. The peace that Jesus offers is indeed human peace, and that is why his love took on a human form and his peace put on a human dress. What the nations need most urgently is a Peace Conference with the Prince of Peace. At such a conference, the world leaders will realise that the peace of God that flows through Christ is far greater than the petty peace they can achieve by themselves. Even we as individuals, when touched by this peace, will easily recognise that Christ's peace is unlike the forced peace that can only be achieved, say, by alcohol; that it is unlike the peace which comes from escaping responsibility through frantic pursuit of pleasures; that it is unlike the superficial joy of prosperity, suggested by slick television commercials. The peace of Christ is very precious, so precious that no money could buy it. Even if it could - just imagine what a luxury tax there would be on it!

Therefore let us make space in our hearts for the peace of Christ to flow in. We make space by becoming ever more sensitive to the presence of the Holy Spirit in and around us, like Elizabeth who at the sight of Mary was touched by the Spirit so deeply she cried out in joy, 'Blessed are you among women' (Lk 1:42).

We make space, by entrusting all our cares to the Lord with a trust like that of Mary who was 'blessed for she trusted that the Lord's words to her would be fulfilled' (Lk 1:45). And we make space, by erecting within our hearts, an interior Castle of Prayer, which the storms of life may beat, but without disturbing the serene quiet within.

The Prince of Peace is sure to enter into such a space made sacred during Advent. His peace will start coming like the morning dew dropping slow, but soon will flow like a river, inundating our whole self with its blessedness, until we in turn become instruments of peace. Christ's peace is not passive, like that which you can find in the grave. His peace is active, urging us to offer the hand of friendship to all and even pressing us to go into the world, not to buy peace by compromising with evil, but to win peace by resisting evil, especially the evil of injustices, for justice and peace are inseparable. Hence, as long as for millions in the world peace means a piece of bread, true peace will elude us; but once justice is done to all, love which is the soul of peace, will flourish; and the peace of Christ will break out, so that nation can speak peace with nation.

Let us pray.

Lord, we pray for the power to be gentle; the strength to be forgiving; the patience to be understanding, and the endurance to accept the consequence of holding to what we believe to be right.

May we put our trust in the power of God to overcome evil, and the power of love to overcome hatred.

We pray for the vision to see and faith to believe in a world emancipated from violence,

a new world where fear shall no longer lead men to do injustice nor selfishness make them bring suffering to others.

Help us to devote our whole life, thought and energy to the task of making peace, praying always for inspiration and the power to fulfil the destiny for which we and all men were created.

Week of prayer for World Peace, 1978

Christmas Day - a third look

HAIL, CHILD JESUS

Isaiah 9:1-6, Titus 2:11-14; Luke 2:1-14

Theme: Hail Child Jesus, God in human flesh, who has made his dwelling among us in order to guide us with his light, fill us with his peace and save us for eternal life.

HAIL CHILD JESUS, OUR LORD AND GOD. 'You are heir of all things, through whom God created all things, the reflection of the Father's Glory. (Heb 1:3). All things bright and beautiful, all things wise and wonderful, you are the God who made them. Mighty is your power that makes one tiny star to guide the mariner from afar. Marvellous is your wisdom that ripens fruit and golden grain; great is your heart that sends sunshine and rain on both the good and the bad. You are unapproachable, yet your height enables you to stoop; Your holiness is undefiled, yet you can handle hearts that droop.

Hail Child Jesus, the Saviour of the world. In you 'the grace of God has appeared offering salvation to all' (Tit 2:11). Yes, even to people of today, who have split the atom, conquered space and birthed new life inside a test tube, you the baby in the manger are the only salvation. It is you who saved us from sin's penalty, its power and presence. We receive salvation free, for you have paid. If only the world could believe this! We go forward in sophistication while falling backward in belief. The God who sent you on earth to bring all people back to Himself, must be full of pity as He watches many still searching for a saviour.

Hail Child Jesus. 'The people who walked in darkness have seen in you a great light' (Is 9:1). If we once lose this light, then it is perpetual night. You are funny. Sometimes you put us in the dark, to prove that you are light. The restless millions waited for this light, whose dawn made all things new. Even though we know that it is better to be saved by a lighthouse than by a lifeboat, we prefer to remain in the dark and lose our course. How often we have followed false lights and when their glow was gone, our pride still struck sparkles of its own. Lead kindly light, when our light is low, when the blood creeps and the nerves prick. Reach down to our sunless days and help us, that instead of cursing the darkness we may light a candle.

Hail Child Jesus. 'Your name is Prince Of Peace' (Is 9:4). Your peace is hard and bitter, for you shed blood to win it. The world too offers peace, but always with a worm in it; your peace is pure and bliss. Give us that peace. We know that our bodies will one day be buried in peace; but our problem is our heart, which is restless now. May our world know, that even if it has to go to war for justice's sake, the purpose of all war must be peace; anything short of it is brutality, futility and stupidity. Give us your peace, so that we can break the shell of unforgiveness in our hearts and be reconciled with one another in peace.

Hail Child Jesus, you are a child of beauty and a joy for ever. At your birth the angel announced 'tidings of great joy' to be shared by the whole people (Lk 2:10). We see heaven in your manger, in fact something greater than heaven, for heaven itself is your handiwork. You give us joy in retrospect as we remember all your gifts in the past. You give us the joy of aspect for there is always some aspect of the present that makes us happy; You give us the joy of prospect as we look forward to the future. Your joy is far richer than the wild joys of living. Give us the joy of the peaceful conscience and of the grateful heart; the joy of the teachable mind and of the glowing hope.

Hail Child Jesus. You are 'the Word become flesh and made your dwelling among us' (Jn 1:14). You dwell among us not only in the tabernacles of our temples, but also in the temple of our hearts; not only in the marvellous nature and beauty of people, but also in the poverty of a slum and in the mud of a battlefield. You dwell among us not only in times of success and good fortune, but also when we are sick and handicapped. You dwell among us in order to transform any situation into a place of your glory; thus our kitchens become our cathedrals, factories become temples, our classrooms become our shrines and our hospitals become heaven. We need your continued presence among us, for we live in a world being torn to pieces by the storm of human passions. Be with us therefore to calm our restless thoughts to silence and to conform our spirits to your image.

Let us pray.

We thank you, God our Father: you have revealed to us your love, you have told us the secret of life in your Child Jesus.

We give you thanks, our Father: you whose name is holy, have visited and hallowed us through your Child Jesus.

Praise to you for creating the Universe, so that the human race can find food and drink; but you have given us the food of eternal Life, your Child Jesus.

Remember us your children, deliver us from evil and confirm us in your love.

Gather your Church from the four winds into the Kingdom you have prepared. Glory to you for ever.

Eucharistic prayer from Didache: 1st-2nd century

1st Sunday of Lent, C

WE ARE IN LENT

Deuteronomy 26:4-10; Romans 10:8-13; Luke 4:1-13

Theme: Lent is a time of spiritual preparation for Easter, purifying our actions and motives from spiritual obstacles and participating in the Passion and Death of Christ through self-sacrifices, in the belief that, with Christ, we will rise again.

Lent is PREPARATION. The loftiest edifices need the deepest foundations. So too, the celebration of the most sublime paschal mystery of the death and resurrection of Jesus Christ needs solemn spiritual preparation. As Israel prepared for forty years before entering into the promised land, Jesus prepared for forty days (Lk.4:1), to enter into his public ministry, which led him to death on the cross; so we prepare during Lent, in order to enter into the depth of Christ's Passion and then into the fairest garden of the purest Easter joy. We prepare by intensive prayer; to us, prayer ought not to be what dolls are to children, just comforting. We must take prayer seriously, at least during Lent, and find time to be alone with God in solitude, for solitude is the audience chamber of God. We prepare through frequent attendance at Mass and the reception of the Sacrament of Reconciliation. Particularly, we prepare through daily meditation on God's word. The word of God is not to be adored only as a monument over the graves of Christians. It needs to be engraved in our hearts, while we are still alive.

Lent is PURIFICATION. If we want to be friends with God, as in all friendships, we have to keep it in constant repair. We have to get rid of those spiritual obstacles which hinder us from responding fully to God's love. We must try to remove even our small faults, for we stumble on stones, not on mountains. Our actions need purification. If we give priority to the physical rather than spiritual, we deny, that 'A man does not live by bread alone' (Lk.4:4). Not only the end of our actions but the means we use to obtain them must be also good. Jesus refused to cast himself down from the pinnacle of the Temple (Lk.4:12), for that was not God's way to make his mission a success. Life is not a football game, where you may be careful about the goal but indifferent to the ball. Above all, the motives for our actions need purification. The true motives of our actions are usually concealed like the pipes of an organ.

Lent is PARTICIPATION. We will fast in Lent. Many of us would deny ourselves some of our cherished pleasures, as a penance, for wanting in the past more than our fair share of the good things in life, even though 140,000 children in the world will die of hunger in the next three days. Some of us will give up part of our comforts to the homeless. We will make all these and many other sacrifices, not out of duty, for even gold is worthless if given out of duty, but as our loving participation in the Passion and Death of our Lord. Yes, if we are to be remade, reborn and turned around, we must first be broken to pieces. For a Christian, who does not daily take Christ's death to himself, the crucifix becomes simply a decoration on the wall. After all, suffering does not have the last word. Those who suffer in union with Christ on the cross, suffer to end all suffering.

Lent is PROCLAMATION. In Lent we proclaim that 'God

who brought our forefathers out of of Egypt with a strong hand and outstretched arms' (Deut 26:8), will bring us also to freedom through the cross of His Son, for it was on the cross that freedom's battle against evil was won. Throughout Lent we profess our faith that, 'Jesus is the Lord who died and rose from the dead' (Rom 10:9), not only to break our chains here and now, but also finally to lead us into the land of the free and the home of the brave. Without this faith, penance will be preposterous. Hence during Lent we must cling to faith, not to just the forms of faith. Faith is not a feeling but a conviction. At times one wonders whether the best among Christians lack all conviction, while the worst in the world are full of passionate intensity. With an active faith and fire within, Lent can offer us a new beginning and it is never too late to begin. It is better to begin in the evening, than not at all.

Let us pray.

O Lord, who for our sake did pray and fast for forty days in the desert, give us grace to use this Lenten observance to subdue our flesh to the Spirit, so that, we may ever obey your godly inspirations. Inspire repentance for our sins and free us from our past.

You created the human race and are the author of its renewal: be with us through this season and all our earthly days, so that, continually renewed through the mystery of your grace, we can join in heaven's praise when the final Easter dawns.

2nd Sunday of Lent, C

THE BEST IS YET TO BE

Genesis 15:5–18, Philippians 3:17–4:1 Luke 9:28–36

Theme: Those who listen to God's Son Jesus and follow him in suffering and death for the sake of love, will be one day led into mankind's glorious destiny.

Our promises made in storms are often forgotten in calms, even if it was a good mouth-filling promise. A doctor said to his patient, 'You will pull through, but you are a very sick man'. The patient replied, 'Please, doctor, do everything you can for me. If I get well, I will donate thirty thousand pounds to the fund for the new hospital'. Several months later, when the patient was completely well, the doctor reminded him: 'You said that if you got well, you would donate thirty thousand pounds?' The former patient exclaimed, 'If I said that, then really I must have been sick'. God's promises are not like ours. He made a promise to Abraham that he would have a great progeny and possess a land of full and plenty' (Gen 15:5) and He did fulfil it. Ordinarily the weaker partner in a contract has to accept more obligations than the stronger one. But in the covenant with Abraham, it was God who bore the brunt of obligations, promising that independent of the faithfulness of the other party, He would be faithful.

God is at His best in faithfulness. When we were captives to sin, He sent His Son as He had promised, who made captivity

2nd Sunday of Lent, C

itself captive, so that we can now enjoy freedom; a freedom which has a thousand charms that slaves never know, including the freedom to enter one day into eternal life. Yes, men tore up the roads that led to heaven and Jesus came to make ladders to it. It is into the open face of this heaven, that the disciples had a sweet glimpse when Jesus was transfigured on Mount Tabor (Lk.9:29), and that was a sneak preview of our own resurrection to come, when 'He will change our weak mortal bodies and make them like his own glorious body'(Phil 13:21). But the road we all have to take to our glorious destiny passes over the Bridge of Sighs, as Jesus himself had to pass through passion and death into his glory; a subject of discussion between Moses and Elijah on mount Tabor (Lk.9:31). The same is true for us. No pain, no palm; no thorns, no throne; no gall, no glory; no cross, no crown.

There is no-one in the world without their daily cross, though they be a king or pope. Life is full of trials and tribulations; even when things go well, they are still going poorly, for we are all growing old. All of us must expect some trouble in life. The guy whose troubles are all behind him is probably a school bus driver.

Everyone has a problem; if there is one who has none, you will find him in the cemetery. Just before Jesus went up the Mount, he asked his followers to carry their daily cross and even lose their lives for his sake, so that they could save them; and on the Mount God said, 'Listen to him' (Lk 9:35). Do we listen? Some people are born deaf, in others hearing is impaired, but there are those whose hearing is nearly perfect but would never listen, with the result 'their lives make them enemies of the cross of Christ' (Phil 3:18). But to a Christian who listens, the cross would not be a mystery but a revelation; for it discloses how much God loves us, and how much we too should love God by embracing our daily cross.

We say we love God and try to love our neighbour, as Christ has loved us. But love is not love until it is vulnerable. Love is essentially sacrificial and that is why the greatest love is a mother's, then comes a dog's, then comes a sweetheart. Besides, when we embrace crosses out of love, we are not suffering for nothing. That would be tragic, for the greatest pain is to love in vain. Through our crosses we are destined to a transformation, similar to that of Christ on Mount Tabor.

Though our bodies be disfigured now on earth with many defects, they will one day be transfigured. But God's promise is that He will lead us to our dazzling destiny not necessarily through crucifixion on the cross, but by daily sacrifices for love.

When some one encourages us, our capacity to achieve our goal expands. Likewise, may this promise of God, uplift our spirits to their fullest potential, for the Best Is Yet To Be.

Let us pray
God our Father, you bid us listen to your Son, the well-beloved;
Nourish our hearts on your word, purify the eye of our mind,
and fill us with joy at the vision of your glory.
Restore our sight that we may look upon your Son
who calls us to repentance and a change of heart.
To strengthen your disciples for coming strife, you climbed the heights
and showed them heaven's light, May that same light shine upon us
so that we may seek nothing but Christ during these lenten days.
Teach us to discipline our body for the good of the soul, and
to set our hearts on fulfilling your precepts.
May we step from the past and walk away from darkness
seeking new paths in the light of heaven.

3rd Sunday of Lent, C

TURN OR BURN

Exodus 3: 1-15: I Corinthians 10: 1-12; Luke 13:1-9

Theme: God whose name is Goodness, also has a limit to His patience and hence waits for us to turn away from sins, lest we are burnt by our own evil.

A LADY ON A TRANSATLANTIC FLIGHT in a jet became very upset when they hit violent turbulence. She asked the stewardess, 'Are we going to crash?' The stewardess tried to calm her down, saying 'Don't be afraid, we are all in the hands of God'. The lady exclaimed 'Oh, is it that bad?', to which the stewardess replied 'No, it is actually that good'. Yes, God is good. He is always good. How many times in the past have we gone to God, for we could go nowhere else, and learnt that the storms of life had driven us, not upon the rocks, but on to a bed of blessings? As it is in the glimpse of darkened skies, that we realise the beauty of the day, so in the daily cares we face, we often come to realise, how much God cares. God gave Moses as His name, 'I AM WHO AM' (Ex 3:14), which may have other meanings, but surely it means that God was, is and will be good to us.

It is not surprising then that we who are the recipients of the goodness of God are expected to respond to God's call with ae similar goodness of heart. When we were baptised into Christ as Israel was into Moses (1 Cor 10:2), God called us to put on the mind and heart of Christ. How can our heart be like that of

Christ who warned us against too much preoccupation with this world, if its desires (1 Cor 10:6) are as greedy as the jaws of hell, with a restless ambition never at an end? How can we reflect the mind of Christ, who came to serve and not to be served, if we sell our souls to self-love, the greatest of flatterers, while our heart for others is as hard-boiled as an Easter egg? How can we say that we drink from the rock of Christ (1 Cor 10:6) who forgave wrongs darker than death, if we store up grudges in the back of our heads as ancient relics? We say that Christ is our way, but when the way becomes bare and rough, we start 'grumbling' (1 Cor 10:7), which soon grows to a mighty rumbling.

We all need, therefore, to repent and change. What destroys us is not ruthless killing such as that inflicted by Pilate on a number of Galileans, as they prepared for worship; nor some construction accident, such as the one that occured at the tower of Siloam; but our unwillingness to repent. So Jesus warns: 'If you do not turn from your sins, you will all die as they did' (Lk 13:1-5). We must accept that most people do repent of their sins, but only by thanking God that they are not so wicked as their neighbour. If we compared our wickedness with the goodness of God, all of us would surely repent and our contrition will certainly become April violet, filling the rest of the year with buds and blossoms.

God is patient, hoping that we would reform ourselves at least during this Lent, a chance He gives once more. But a doctor who tries a medicine a certain number of times but finds no change abandons the use of the drug. As there is a limit to every effort, so there is limit to God's patient waiting. If we do not produce, at least during Lent, fruits in personal growth, prayer and community service, God may have to 'cut down the fig tree to be burnt' (Lk 3:-5). However, reform is not possible all by ourselves. We need grace and we cannot get grace from gadgets but only from God. Hence we must come to God in prayer during this period of grace. God will hear our prayers, as He heard those of Israel and delivered them (Ex 3:17). If some of our prayers in the past were not answered, probably we put too many commercials into them. But a prayer for conversion will surely be heard. Our faces may be filled with broken commandments and our hearts with sins, as dark as night. Still, we must not hesitate to come to God, for God knows how to make use of our sins as manure for the Tree of Life. Hence, to the Lord let us turn, lest we burn.

Let us pray
O Sun of Justice, fill our hearts where sinfulness has brought decay;
Dispel the darkness of our souls as now the night gives place to day.

Make this a fitting time for us, a time to change and turn to you;
Please hear our prayer, most patient Lord, Repentance in our hearts renew.

As spring awakes the frozen earth, so Easter blooms from Lent's restraints.

Rejoice! for Christ will conquer death and bring his grace to make us saints

Latin hymn, 6th century

4th Sunday of Lent, C

A NEW CREATION - A NEW WORLD

Joshua 5:9-12; 2 Cor 5:17-21; Luke 15:1-3,11-32

Theme: Since our true happiness lies in belonging to our Father's house and to the Family of man, we are called to return to God and our fellow people and be made in Christ new creations for a new world.

A WIDOW WHO HAD SPENT LONG HOURS AND DAYS in the factory and at home, raising her four children, lay exhausted and emaciated on her deathbed. Around her stood the four of them, now grown up men and women. The eldest son, in tears, said to her, 'Mother, you have always been so good and kind to us. We want to thank you. We are proud of you'. The mother opened her eyes and asked, 'Why have you waited so long to tell me that? You never ever said so before'. She turned her head away and died. All of us love children, for they are like olive branches around a table, but some of them can be utterly ungrateful. When the younger son in the parable of the prodigal demanded from his father the portion of his estate (Lk 15:12), his intention was not to insult his father, yet it was like telling him to drop dead. The father, though shattered by this impulsive brashness, still gave him the money. The son left his father's house taking on the world alone, only to come crashing down with a painful bang.

It is a warning to those of us who have either left or are leaving our Father and His house; the Family of Humankind. Our true happiness lies in belonging to our Father's house. Do we really belong to God our Father? Have we not all been unfaithful to Him at some times, making totally inadequate response to His love and 'squandering' (Lk 15:13) at least some of our heritage? Do we truly belong to the house of our Father, which is human society, by our loving care and brotherly concern for each other? Perhaps some of us are like the elder brother of the parable, withdrawn, unapproachable, bitter and afraid to mix with others, finding our security in excessive devotion to duty and earning money. To belong to a particular human society may be a bore, but to be out of it is simply a tragedy; for we were formed for society and one would not be alone, even in paradise.

All of us have gone astray in some sense and need to return to our Father's house. God will surely receive us, for He is not just good but reckless in His goodness. He will be good to us, whether we are like the younger son: a prodigal, or like the elder son: a paranoid. When we return to Him, let us bring with us that lost part of ourselves which God has been tracking down; once we are reconciled whole and entire with God and neighbour, we will discover that we have returned to a heaven of peace and new beginning. How our hearts, at times, yearn for that land of new beginnings, where all our mistakes and headaches could be dropped like a shaggy coat at the door, never to be put on again! Indeed, God has provided us with such a land in the heart of His Son Jesus. In the past, God 'removed from Israel the shame of slavery' (Jos 5:9) and now, through Christ's death on the cross, He has freed us from sin; Hence, 'if anyone is in Christ, he is a new creation' (2 Cor 5:1).

New creation, indeed, we became at baptism, but as a new broom is said to be good only for three days, so we lose our newness in Christ soon and often by our sins. However, at the sacrament of Reconciliation our merciful Father again and again welcomes us to reconcile with himself and with His community, appealing earnestly that we in turn become 'ministers of reconciliation' who can 'reconcile the world to God' (2 Cor 5:18). This means that we become New Creations, so that we can work for a new world!

We are forgiven, so that we can not only forgive others but even forget their offences; for it is better to forget and smile than to remember and be sad. It is forgiveness that reveals the power of love and it is love that brings about peace. We may call for peace as loudly as we can, but where there is no love, there can be no peace. It is peace, not battle that tests the Christian strength, because peace is a daily process, slowly eroding old barriers and quietly building new bridges.

Let us pra.y
Our Father, we have wandered and hidden from your face;
In foolishness we have squandered your legacy of grace.
But now, in exile dwelling, we rise with fear and shame,
as distant but compelling, we hear you call our name.

And now at length discerning, the evil that we do
behold us, Lord, returning with hope and trust in you.
In haste you come to meet us and home rejoicing bring
in gladness there to greet us with calf, robe and ring.

Kevin Nichols

5th Sunday of Lent, C

IT IS HAPPENING AGAIN

Is 43:16-21; Phil 3:8-14; Jn 8:1-11

Theme: The mercy of God is calling us back to drink the waters of life, that flow from Christ at the sacrament of reconciliation, as He did to the people of Israel in the past and to the penitent sinners during the life of Christ.

IT HAPPENED TO THE PEOPLE OF ISRAEL IN THE PAST. Who does not know the appalling miseries and sleepless sufferings they bore? It is true, pleasures too visited them, but remember, pain and cruelty clung to them. However, every time they fell upon the thorns of life, God, the great cloud of mercy, rained compassion to quench the fire that burned their lives. God, the mighty liberator, parted the waters of the Red Sea for them. The God who worked wonders during their Exodus from Egypt, seven centuries later worked a new wonder to bring about their return from Babylonian captivity, saying, 'See, I am doing something new. Now it springs forth, do you not perceive it? In the desert I make a way, in the wastelands rivers' (Is 43:9). Who among us can smile in the face of adversity and mean it? So the chosen people cried to God every time calamity hit them, and He came to pluck the burden of sorrow from them.

It happened to penitent sinners during the life of Christ. Christ was the reaching out of God to sinful humanity. That is why, when others wanted to condemn and kill the woman caught in adultery, Jesus forgave her, saying, 'I do not condemn you' (Jn 8:11). If Jesus overtook even the flying eagle to embrace every sinner, it was because he was the Sacrament of God, the ocean of boundless compassion. The sinners Jesus forgave were only representing the whole of humanity, for all have sinned. When the Pharisees brought the woman, accusing her of sin, Jesus said, 'Let the one among you who has no sin be the first. to cast a stone at her' (Jn 8:7). Jesus looked down at the earth and doodled in it with his fingers, reminding us that all of us are sinners; for dust is the origin and destiny of our bodies. But Jesus does not write our sins on rock to remain for ever, but on dust, to be blown away by the mercy of God, who does not snuff out the smouldering wick or beat the bruised reed.

It is happening again to us here and now, in the sacrament of confession, where the merciful Lord continues to forgive our slns. Many people for various reasons have stopped going to confession. For some, sin is not real; if it is not, why did Jesus say to the woman, ' Go, sin no more' (Jn.8:11)? Others make excuses for their sins, appealing to Sociology or Psychology, as for example when they justify pre-marital sex as a necessary experience for growth in maturity, although they know that it is better to have a fool to make us merry than an experience to make us sad. Still others find no use in confession, for they have to repeat the same faults again and again. But don't we go to the doctor over and over again for shots or medicine, if we know, that we are born with some physical allergies? All of us have some inborn spiritual weaknesses, because of which we fail again and again. Why then should we worry about repeating our faults to the good Lord? After all, repetition is everywhere and nothing is found only once in the world.

Hence, the mercy of God is calling us back to drink the waters of life that flow from Christ. Are we ready to return and open ourselves to God's love? The greatest sin is not adultery but deliberately closing our minds and hearts to God's love and closing in on oneself and away from others in pride and self-sufficiency. In fact we are called to be as enthusiastic in our return to the Lord, as St Paul was who said, 'I have accounted all else rubbish, so that Christ can be my wealth' (Phil 3:5). If we do come to the Lord, we will enter into the Palace of Love, where the treasures of the King are kept with all the kisses of love. Kissed by love, we will have truth, which is on the side of the oppressed today. We will have integrity, which baffles those full of duplicity; We will have mercy, which blesses the one who gives and the one who takes; and we will have courage, which narrow souls dare not admire.

Let us pray.
Lord, graciously hear us, hear us as we call on you;
we tried to be faithful, Lord, but we have sinned against you.

You gave us your message, you showed us the way to live:
we tried to be faithful, Lord, but we have not understood.

Lord, show us your mercy, heal those we have wounded here;
we wanted to love like you, but we have forgotten the way.

Speak, Lord, to your people, speak now in a million way;s
we want to be true to you, help and forgive us, we pray.

Anne Conway

Passion Sunday, C

CHRIST REIGNS FROM THE CROSS

Isaiah 50:4-7; Philippians 2:6-11 Luke 23:1-49

Theme: Because the cross on which Christ chose to die became a throne from which he would reign over sin and death, we too can win crown and glory, through our cross and pain.

EVEN A COLD, UNTROUBLED HEART OF STONE will pause to breathe, and a noble heart will certainly crack, at the sufferings of Christ during his Passion. After being let down by his friends and betrayed by some; after suffering frightening anguish in Gethsemane, after being tried for the offences he did not commit; and after being taunted by blows, spits, lashes of whip and piercing of thorns, he was finally crucified on the cross. On the cross, he was stabbed with nails of black iron, causing gushing wounds, the gaping marks of malice. Clouds of darkness covered his body with blackness. They mutilated his body, the lovely casket of his soul.

His death was the most dreadful of all deaths, for he was both Son of God and Son of Man. His sufferings were real, not play-acting, for he was not made of some super flesh, insensitive to pain, nor of a super-soul which served as anaesthetic. Anyone who doubts that his sufferings were real challenges Christ's honesty.

However, the cross upon which Christ freely chose to die became a throne from which he would reign. There was never a fairer morning than the golden dawn of Easter Day when he rose; there never was a greater joy, than the stunning moment when the angels affirmed that he lives again; there never came a nobler hope that we are immortal and our life surges towards inifinity since Christ died and rose for all. Christ reigns from the cross, because, after entering into our sinful state, he twisted sin's own weapon, death, out of its grasp and used it as a means for humanity to return to God. Christ reigns from the cross, because the cross upon which he was the Suffering Servant of the Lord, transformed him into the Son of Glory. Christ reigns from the cross, because the cross that gathered together all the sorrows in the world into the one Sorrow of Christ, in a moment of utter defeat won complete victory over all human sorrows.

Therefore, no tree in all the wood is dearer to us Christians than the tree of the cross. It reminds us that we too can win crown and glory through cross and pain. At times pain pricks us, at other times it hurts us like hell or a crack on our heads with a whip. We find our personal calvaries even in our homes and communities, as the result of the violence and harm we do to each other. Some of us place others on the cross by our hatred and rejection of them. And there are communal calvaries, called Social Structures, created by the unjust, supported by the violent, exploited by the greedy and abused by the powerful. However, in our suffering, if we jump to the crucified feet of Christ, like a wounded deer that leaps highest, he will console and comfort us and fill our cups to overflowing; for his rivers of might and mercy are all broad. Besides, the same cross which we daily embrace on this earth will one day bid us to leave this fleeting life, to sit at the banquet of the Lord in heaven.

Until that day of glory, when God will look us over, we will bear our sufferings as Christ did, not for medals but for scars. Christ suffered for love. Our renunciations and sacrifices will be worthless without love, as all the coal and firewood in the world are useless without fire. Christ showed compassion, even to his executioners. Likewise, we who cannot do anything with sin, can do at least something with suffering, namely, we can take it from others upon ourselves. Christ did not indulge in self-pity during his pains. We may win compassion through self-pity, but the pity of it is that every horse thinks his own pack heaviest. Above all, Christ suffered with hope that God would raise him. So too, we in our sufferings, whether they come singly or in battalions, must hope that they are the means to find our homeward way to our glorious destiny. He who daily puts forth such tender leaves of hope, will surely see them one day blossom.

Let us pray.

Lord Jesus, your cross is splendid, for it brings life, not death; light, not darkness; paradise, not loss.

It is the wood on which you were wounded, but you healed thereby our wounds.

One tree in the garden destroyed us, but another on Calvary brought us life.

We venerate your cross, from which we draw great mercy.

Help us to keep always in mind, that you died for us but rose from the dead; so too:, if we die with you, we shall also live with you and if we endure with you, we shall also reign with you.